TEXAS INDIAN TRAILS

TEXAS INDIAN TRAILS

Daniel J. Gelo and Wayne J. Pate

REPUBLIC OF TEXAS PRESS

Dallas • Lanham • Boulder • New York • Toronto • Oxford

Published by Republic of Texas Press
An imprint of The Rowman & Littlefield Publishing Group, Inc.
4501 Forbes Boulevard, Suite 200
Lanham, MD 20706

Distributed by NATIONAL BOOK NETWORK

Library of Congress Cataloging-in-Publication Data

Gelo, Daniel J., 1957–
    Texas Indian trails / Daniel J. Gelo and Wayne J. Pate.
        p.   cm.
    Includes bibliographical references and index.
    ISBN 1-55622-895-3 (alk. paper)
    1. Indians of North America—Texas—History—Guidebooks.   2. Indians of North America—Texas—Antiquities—Guidebooks.   3. Texas—Guidebooks.
I. Pate, Wayne.   II. Title.
    E78.T4G45 2003
    917.6404′64—dc21
                                                        2002008928

CONTENTS

ACKNOWLEDGMENTS

The authors offer warm thanks to Ginnie Siena Bivona at Republic of Texas Press for putting us on the trail in a big way. Our appreciation also goes to Jatin Bhavsar, Julia Chindemi, Beatrice Delgado, Lisa Garcia, Gene Hopstetter, Jason Hayes, and Dr. Richard Wenzlaff, all at the University of Texas, San Antonio, for assisting with research and photo and map preparation. We also salute Janice Braunstein, Jessica Gribble, Scott Jerard, and Elizabeth Weiss of Rowman and Littlefield for their fine work in bringing out this book.

Dan Gelo wishes to thank Fred and Kay Campbell, John Crain, Dan Flores, Richard Francaviglia, Elizabeth A. H. John, Hoppy Hopkins, Linda Pelon, Robert Reitz, and Gardner Smith, for sharing their enthusiasm and knowledge of the Native landscape. Always generous with their expertise and hospitality have been many members of the Alabama-Coushatta, Comanche, Delaware, Kickapoo, Kiowa, and Tigua tribes. In particular, Jack Battise, George and Tammy Blackowl, Vernon and Gloria Cable, Walter Celestine, Rudy Colmenero, Linda Durant, Herbert Johnson Jr., Thomas Wayne Keahbone, the late Ralph Kosechata, Floyd and Glenna Pekah, Carney Saupitty, Tomas Silvas, the late Cora Sylestine, Margaret

Thomas, and the late Thomas Wahnee deserve more gratitude than can be expressed for their friendships and guidance over the last twenty years. Added thanks to Gabrielle, Terence, and Thomas Gelo for their forbearance during all the traveling and writing.

Wayne Pate thanks Mike Blakely for urging him to attend the Western Writers of America conference; for moral and logistical support, he wishes to express gratitude to Denman and Jackie Pate, Korina Pate, Grant Pate, Clyde and Ann Marie Heminger, Irma Fey, Rafael Sustaita, Rudy and Emily Purificato, George and Norman Russell, and Ann Burton. Wayne is also grateful to Dr. Robert Milk, Dr. Carolyn Kessler, and his other colleagues in Bicultural–Bilingual Studies at the University of Texas, San Antonio, for the employment opportunities that allowed time to pursue research and writing. Special thanks are also offered to Ben Tahmahkera, Baldwin Parker Jr., Don Parker, and Jaquetta Parker McClung of the Comanche Nation for sharing Comanche perspectives on landscape and the world of Quanah Parker. Thanks, too, for the hospitality and helpfulness of numerous persons encountered while seeking out sites.

Finally, the authors thank each other for sharing in the enjoyable effort of reimagining the landscape.

INTRODUCTION

You may already be aware of some landmarks, trails, or campsites that date back to the days when Indian people roamed freely over the land that became Texas. Chances are that there are more such places not far from your home, and many others within a day's drive. The Texas landscape takes on a new immediacy when you visit known Indian places. The land provides us with a fresh appreciation for the rich historical heritage of Texas and the Native Americans who have lived here.

Conversely, deeper knowledge of Texas's colorful past prompts us to value the land in a new way. No place has more potential for teaching the historical significance of the landscape than Texas, and nowhere are the lessons greater: The story of Texas is the story of the West, and the saga of Indians in Texas encapsulates the Native experience all across America.

REDISCOVERING THE TEXAS NATIVE AMERICAN LANDSCAPE

It is probably fair to say that virtually every spring and sheltering hillside in Texas has seen some Indian activity in the twelve thousand years of human occupation of the state. Among these are numerous places that Indians are definitely known to have used or inhabited, in addition to others that can be noted as probable sites with more than the usual degree of confidence. Evidence for Indian activity on the landscape comes from many sources. The knowledge passed down verbally among non-Indian ranchers and other landowners is a starting point. These memories have been frequently written down in the local and regional histories published by towns and counties. Spanish and American military reports as well as the journals of explorers and surveyors also record Indian camping places and landmarks.

The discoveries of archaeologists, published in site reports, may confirm prior reports or add new knowledge. Though it is too often forgotten, Indian people themselves are an excellent source of primary information about Native land use in Texas. Indians of the past produced numerous pictorial works, including rock paintings that still exist at several Texas sites. Other such items include the Kiowa tribe's calendar histories (yearly records painted on buffalo hide), which show Indian people using certain locations at specific times. Modern tribe members often have remarkably detailed knowledge of their ancestors' land use practices, passed down in legend, and this traditional information, although not totally new to scholars, often meshes with data from the other sources mentioned.

A good deal of the primary source information has been gathered in articles and books, but these works are either too specialized or too general to be used easily by history-minded travelers. Gunnar Brune's classic work, *The Springs of Texas*, synthesizes much useful information about Indian use of water sources around the state.

Most of what is known about historical Alabama and Coushatta trails and campsites comes to us through the diligent research of Howard Martin, while coauthor Daniel J. Gelo has published numerous articles on the Comanche sense of place. The entries in *Why Stop?* (Awbrey, Dooley, and Texas Historical Commission, 1978), a compendium of Texas historical marker texts, and the Texas Historical Commission's *New Handbook of Texas* contain many of the facts about Indian occupation of particular places in the state.

Texas Indian Trails is the first book, however, to do all of the following: bring together all of the in-print information about Texas Indian trails and campsites; assess this material critically; add original field research; and make it all manageable for travelers and other general readers. All prior published sources used in preparing *Texas Indian Trails* are listed in the bibliography at the end of the book. This list is meant to acknowledge previous writers in the absence of item-by-item citations within the text, and it is also intended as a guide for those readers who would like further background about the places discussed here.

The main purpose of *Texas Indian Trails* is to provide dependable information about the established travel routes, landmarks, and campsites used by the Indians of Texas, in a manner that will enliven travels around the state. We want to make this information accessible in one place, and we want to make it useful to a wide range of nonspecialist readers, including those with the energy to go driving to see for themselves.

A related goal is simply to preserve the Native American part of Texas history and to broaden public understanding about it. We also hope the book will inspire preservationist interest in natural features of the landscape that is comparable to the devotion currently given to certain historical buildings and famous people. As the population of Texas continues to expand, it will be important to guard against the obliteration of those natural places that are historically significant, though perhaps not obviously so.

Another aim of ours is to show just how heavy the Indian legacy is in modern Texas geography; place names and the locations of contemporary towns and roads are often directly traceable to Indian practices, although this inheritance often goes unrecognized. Finally, we hope to draw attention to the living quality of Texas Indian cultures. As chapter 1 shows, even though many people think Texas Indians simply disappeared in the 1800s, there are more people alive today who count ancestry from the Texas tribes than at any time in the historic period. Texas is home to three Indian reservations, and thousands of people throughout Texas, Oklahoma, and the United States perpetuate beliefs and rituals grounded in Native Texas. Their traditions are a great resource for all of us as we seek to better understand the conditions that shape human life in the Lone Star State.

Careful students of Texas Indian history will notice that certain significant places are not covered in *Texas Indian Trails*. Since this book is a roadside guide, some sites that either lie deep within private property or are otherwise not accessible from public roads have not been included. In a few cases, however, we have included places where it is possible to get close enough to an interesting remote site to gain an impression of the landscape (for example, further upstream along the same creek).

The forts that were built to police the Texas frontier often became important centers for Indian–white interaction, peaceful as well as hostile. We have included a few forts when their histories reveal something about the Indian perspective on the land or on unfolding events, but we did not make an effort to treat forts comprehensively. Some other books do: see Aston and Taylor's *Along the Texas Forts Trail* (1997) and Timanus's *An Illustrated History of Texas Forts* (2001).

In general, we have focused on sites known from the historic period, as defined in chapter 1, although we have not cataloged the numerous prehistoric sites charted by archaeologists. A few prehistoric sites—Hueco Tanks, Lubbock Lake, Seminole Canyon, and Caddoan Mounds—have been included because they are well protected, managed, and interpreted; in addition, they are especially good for showing the depth of time of Indian occupation in their respective regions.

HOW TO USE *TEXAS INDIAN TRAILS*

After an overview of all the Texas tribes in chapter 1, the sites are organized in six chapters covering regions of the state: the East, the South, the Hill Country, the Rolling Plains, the Staked Plains, and the Mountains and Basins area. Each region's chapter is formatted the same way. A brief introduction and a "Lay of the Land" section sketch the regional environment and the Native peoples who lived there. Then, each site is identified and explained, and specific directions are given between sites or vantage points. The sites are tied together in a continuous tour of the whole region. We have tried to begin and end the tour of each region as close as possible to the center of the Lone Star State. If a map of Texas were used as a dartboard, the town of Brady would become the center of the bull's-eye. That point has been our primary reference in attempting to begin and end regional routes.

We attempted to make each route as much of a circle as possible; but as we accounted for all the sites, they invariably turned into ragged shapes with occasional detours from a continuous circuit. For a few of the regions, we outlined alternate tour segments. Sometimes the routing dictated that places normally thought of as part of one region be treated under another region (for example, some sites southwest of Fort Worth have been included in the chapter on East Texas). Also, a few sites on the border of two regions were equally well approached from either area and are thus included under both chapters. A map for each region shows all sites and main towns along the route, and we have also included photos of select locations.

Even though good descriptive information is available for many of the sites, any trip to view old Indian trails and camps must be mainly a journey of the imagination. Many of the places this book will take you to will not stand out unless you can populate them with imaginary Indians, horses, and tipis. When you arrive at such places, erase in your mind's eye whatever paved roads, frame buildings, and telephone lines have intruded. Even the more wild and seemingly pristine locations will need the benefit of your historical imagination, for the streams of Texas once ran deeper and clearer, and the vegetation was often different in Indian days. We offer this advice up front, because it is a long drive between many of the sites. While some are stunning, magical places and while all are significant from a historical perspective, not all of them are particularly scenic or dramatic. Tour routes should be studied before departure, and a careful assessment should be made of whether one's curiosity about individual sites will justify the driving time necessary to reach and view them.

To see all the Indian sites of Texas, you'll need a lot of gas and a lot of time. Don't let the distances between sites discourage you, though; those who travel Texas know there is always something intriguing to be found around the next bend, and anyone with the explorer's mind-set will find entertainment in the journeys as well as the destinations. Our circuits connect places in such a way that ambitious travelers could cover an entire region (chapter) in a long holiday weekend. Lodging can be found in the larger towns for overnight trips. Most folks will probably find it easier to select a few sites along the circuits we lay out and see them on day trips. See our recommendations at the end of this introduction for some nice day trips from the major Texas metropolitan areas. If you would like to search out the sites singly or just keep the guide handy in your glove box to check on what you may be passing during routine travel, these tactics will work fine, too.

When actually making a recommended trip, you will want to coordinate the described route with a good road map; or, better, use an atlas that shows detail at the level of county roads, such as *The Roads of Texas* or the *Texas Atlas & Gazetteer* (see the bibliography). To help in your planning, our directions include mileage figures that can be used to judge the length of trips and segments. These mileage figures may not correspond exactly with what is shown on your vehicle's odometer, so treat them only as approximations when you are seeking specific intersections and stopping points. For a few of the sites (state parks, for example), telephone numbers are given. Always call ahead to learn current hours and fees. Although the phone numbers were up to date at the time this book was written, they may have changed; try them, but call information for new numbers when necessary.

It is always a good idea to check your vehicle to see that it is in good repair before beginning a tour. The more sparsely populated and harsher the tour region is, the more crucial this precaution becomes. In many areas of the state, stranded drivers can realistically expect to wait for hours before other travelers pass their way, and many of those who do come by will be understandably wary of stopping for strangers. Take along a wireless phone for added security.

Routes have been selected with the average car in mind, and only rarely does the recommended path take the traveler off paved roads. When routes leave pavement, the stretches are always short and are always on "improved" county roads. These roads, however, can be rough—"washboardy"—and you should travel them slowly to avoid jostling passengers or damaging your vehicle. They can usually be negotiated with confidence, except in times of wet weather or in places covered with deep, loose sand. Only the most sheltered city dweller in Texas is unfamiliar with the term *getting stuck*. Use good judgment, and know what your vehicle can do. (Many drivers who frequent unpaved roads carry a shovel and at least two three-to-four-foot pieces of wood to lay under their drive wheels. With this equipment, delays caused by sand or mud rarely last more than a few minutes.)

It is also smart practice to routinely carry water for drinking or use in your engine. You may also want to include extra engine coolant, food, and clothing. During hunting season (September 1 through mid-May), it is wise to wear a bright hat or shirt when stopping in rural areas. Sunglasses and sunscreen will also come in handy, and binoculars are highly recommended to fully enjoy views of many of the sites.

Anyone with a true explorer's attitude will occasionally be frustrated by the restraints of fences, locked gates, and NO TRESPASSING signs, but these barriers should prove to be no problem for travelers who follow the routes described and who can satisfy themselves with a good look at a camping place or trail, even if some sites are only visible in the distance. As you use *Texas Indian Trails*, please respect the property rights of landowners. Many of the sites we include lie on private property, which may or may not be posted. If you have to wonder whether it is private property, it probably is—so *keep off*.

While state and federal lands may allow you closer access to some sites, remember that these places are protected by laws that prohibit disturbance of natural or cultural features. Texas state law makes it unlawful for anyone to disturb in any way any historic, prehistoric, or archaeological site situated on lands owned or controlled by the state; penalties can be as much as $1,000 plus thirty days in jail. Similar antiquities laws apply on federal lands. Please stay on trails and refrain from taking or moving materials of any kind.

Further information about protecting the prehistoric and historic legacies of Texas places can be obtained by contacting the following sources:

Center for Archaeological Research
University of Texas at San Antonio
6900 North Loop 1604 West
San Antonio, TX 78249
(210) 458-4378
www.csbs3.utsa.edu/car

Texas Historical Commission
P.O. Box 12276
Austin, TX 78711
(512) 463-6100
www.thc.state.tx.us

Texas Parks and Wildlife
4200 Smith School Road
Austin, TX 78744
(800) 792-1112
www.tpwd.state.tx.us

Texas Archaeological Research Laboratory
The University of Texas at Austin
J. J. Pickle Research Campus, Bldg. 5
Austin, TX 78712
(512) 471-5960
www.utexas.edu/research/tarl

Texas Indian Trails can be your guide to many enjoyable drives and to a deeper appreciation of American Indian and Lone Star history. If only for a few fleeting moments, reimagine the landscape as the Native Americans did, and in the process understand better the lives of the earliest Texans.

DAY TRIPS FROM THE HOUSTON AREA

- The easiest and most fruitful day trip involves stops at the sites of Colita's Village, the Old Alabama-Coushatta Campground, the modern Alabama-Coushatta Reservation, Peach-Tree Village, Coushatta Trace, Long Tom's Trace, Long King's Village, Indian Hill, and the Kickapoo Trace (see chapter 2).
- Another day trip north of Houston includes Poole's Creek and the junction of the Brazos and Little Rivers (chapter 2).
- The two trips can be combined into one longer day trip.
- At least three sites from chapter 3—Red Bluff, Linnville, and Blackjack Peninsula—can be seen in a day trip from Houston; with a slightly longer day, Big Hill can also be visited on the return to the city.

DAY TRIPS FROM THE DALLAS–FORT WORTH AREA

From Dallas

If departing from Fort Worth, add at least one hour each way.

- An easy day trip involves a visit to the vicinity of Gilmer to view the Cherokee Trace and Indian Rock (see chapter 2 for more on these sites).
- Equally comfortable is a day trip to the Kilgore/Tyler/Longview area to visit the sites of Cherokee Village, Nadaco Village, and Cherokee Bayou (see chapter 2).
- A more ambitious but still manageable day trip would involve combining the two trips.

- A number of sites clustered in the Waco area are easily approached from Dallas, including Waco Springs, Tehuacana Creek, Torrey's Trading Post, Tehuacana Hills, and Old Fort Parker (see chapter 2).

From Fort Worth, "Where the West Begins"

If departing from Dallas, add one hour each way.

- Any or all of the sites forming a cluster in the area from Bowie north to the Red River can be seen in a day, including Brushy Mound, Queens Peak, Devil's Backbone, and Spanish Fort (see chapter 5).
- Another easy day trip from Fort Worth includes Comanche Peak (see chapter 5) and Johnson Peak and Indian Gap (chapter 2).
- Though much more ambitious than the trips mentioned, a carefully planned day trip can reach the sites around Abilene, including Abilene State Park, Buffalo Gap, and Double Mountain (chapter 5).

I

THE TEXAS TRIBES

T he huge modern state of Texas spans three of the major natural areas of North America that gave rise to distinct Native
American cultural patterns. It includes woodlands typical of eastern
North America, the central prairies and plains, and a southwestern
desert. It is no wonder, then, that Indians were attracted from all
directions to the area that became Texas and that, as they settled
here, they took up different livelihoods, depending on their backgrounds and the particular environments they claimed. Once in the
area, however, Native peoples participated in a continual dynamic
of trade, combat, migration, and displacement that was well under
way before any non-Indians arrived (and when they did arrive, all
such activity was immediately intensified).

   To account for this complex scene, it has become normal to first
distinguish between the prehistoric and historic periods. *Prehistoric*
refers to the times before written records were made, which in Texas
were the days before the coming of Europeans, since none of the
Texas Indians had writing systems—though they certainly had their
own understanding of the past, which was handed down in oral
tradition and pictographs. Most of Indian life in Texas took place
in the prehistoric period, from about twelve thousand until about
five hundred years ago. The study of prehistory is tremendously
important, although it is also very difficult because of the limited
nature of evidence from the distant past.

Prehistorians rely on archaeological evidence—objects and traces of human activity (artifacts) discovered by survey and excavation and interpreted through scientific methods such as classification, and chemical and statistical analysis. Language also provides clues for the prehistorian, since similar Indian languages found in widespread places today reveal patterns of ancient migration. The legends of tribal peoples also contain valuable information about the distant past.

All of these ways of knowing are also relevant to the study of the more recent past; however, in the historic period, they are supplemented with written observations of all kinds: unpublished and published diaries and journals; censuses; newspapers; and reports of soldiers, traders, and missionaries. In the historic period, we know much more detail about Texas Indian life. We are able to name specific tribes and individuals, and we can report their activities, words, motivations, and beliefs—information not easily determined for prehistoric populations.

The following sections provide overviews of the prehistoric and historic Indians of Texas that will help readers better understand the places and events noted in this book (most of the sites documented are historic ones). These sketches make up a handy reference, but bear in mind that they are also very basic; readers are urged to study the abundant writings on the cultures and histories of the various Texas tribes, many of which are listed among our sources in the bibliography.

PREHISTORIC INDIANS OF TEXAS

Paleo-Indians

The culture of the earliest known Indians seems to have been pretty uniform across all of North America. It involved the hunting of big game, mostly animals that have since become extinct: giant bison, camels, sloths, mammoths, mastadons, and early forms of the horse. These creatures lived in parklands (grasslands alternating with

evergreen forest) below the line of polar ice that once extended
into the present northern United States, which comprised conditions that were cooler and wetter than today. The big-game hunters
are known as Paleo-Indians (ancient Indians). They appeared in
Texas around twelve thousand years ago. The evidence of their activity includes certain stone spear points that are sometimes found
with the bones of extinct animals. Examples include Folsom and
Clovis points, which are named for sites in New Mexico, just over
the Texas state line.

Scientists believe that the Paleo-Indians lived in small mobile
bands. They were skillful toolmakers and hunters who may have
been able to take advantage of animals' instincts. One of their favorite techniques was the jump-kill, in which game herds were
chased over a cliff. Such mass kill sites are occasionally found in
Texas—the Bonfire Shelter site outside of Langtry is a well-known
example. Recent studies at other sites show that Paleo-Indians were
also adept at hunting small game and gathering plant foods.

The appearance of the Paleo-Indian homes and clothing remains
speculative. Stone, bone, wood, and hide were the materials they
commanded. However, they had no pottery, which would have been
impractical for mobile hunters, and they also lacked cloth and metal.
Their ethnic units and languages remain mysteries, and it is important to note that the term *Paleo-Indian* is an archaeological term
that refers to a general cultural pattern and not a specific tribe or
linguistic group.

In Texas, the remnants of Paleo-Indian life are sometimes found
beneath the artifacts left by later Indians and non-Indians, indicat-
ing that certain locations have been valued through all the years of
human occupation in the state.

Archaic Peoples

Like the Paleo-Indians, people of the Archaic are not a tribe, but a
group defined by archaeologists according to a time period and the
lifeways associated with that period. Around eight thousand years
ago, the great glaciers melted back, retreating from most of North

America. The environment in Texas changed from fairly uniform parklands to the variety of forests, prairies, swamps, and deserts we see today, though these features were not always in the same places they are now found. The giant fauna became extinct and were replaced by the now-familiar smaller animals—even the modern buffalo is a "dwarf" species compared to its bison ancestors. Indian people thus began to live differently: they adjusted to differing specific environments; they hunted and trapped small game, birds, and fish; and they harvested many kinds of wild plant foods.

The Archaic peoples figured out how to make specialized stone tools—discernable as points, drills, scrapers, net sinkers, or grinding stones—and various inventions that, although simple, were major advances, items such as boats, fish nets, decoys, woven sandals, baskets, and domesticated dogs. The *atlatl,* a lever for throwing short spears called darts, was the main weapon. These inventions allowed Archaic hunter–gatherers to be very successful in living off the land. They developed into much larger groups than the Paleo-Indians did. As dense archaeological remains suggest, some of the groups were able to survive at the same location throughout the year. In addition, they had enough time away from food collecting to devote to art and elaborate ceremonies. The most famous Texas Archaic sites occur around the junction of the Pecos River and Rio Grande, where a dry climate has preserved the rock art and artifacts of thriving Archaic populations who lived in rock shelters and caves above the rivers.

Late Prehistoric Peoples

Abundant small projectile points appear in the Texas archaeological record around thirteen hundred years ago, marking the invention of the bow and arrow and thus the late prehistoric period. Indians of the late prehistoric continued to refine hunting tools and techniques, and traces of their settlements suggest fairly complex social organizations. They also established long-distance trade routes linking Texas with Mexico and the Rocky Mountains, by which they obtained obsidian, volcanic glass treasured for toolmaking because of the sharp edges it can hold. These late prehistoric trade networks were often adopted by invading tribes as the historic period unfolded. They were eventually taken over by non-Indians, thus forming our modern travel routes.

Even more revolutionary than the bow and arrow was the adoption of cultivation. Indians of Texas learned to grow plant foods after corn, originally a wild grass, was domesticated in Central Mexico, and after the idea of farming had spread to the lands east and west of Texas. Horticulture (gardening) and agriculture (farming) furnished more predictable food supplies with surpluses for future insurance, and they both encouraged permanent settlements with large, complexly organized societies. The main Indian crops of corn, beans, and squash form a balanced meal when eaten together. Only some Natives were willing or able to become farmers; the rest continued as hunters and gatherers through the historic period and until they were confined to reservations. Seasonal hunting of buffalo, deer, bear, and small game also remained important for the farming communities.

Although the late prehistoric peoples are not known by their own names, we can see among them populations that were ancestral to named tribes in the historic period. These founder groups include the so-called Early Caddos of East Texas and the Jornado Mogollon, prehistoric Pueblo Indians along the Rio Grande.

HISTORIC INDIAN PEOPLES OF TEXAS

The historic period in Texas could be said to begin with the writings of Cabeza de Vaca, the shipwrecked Spaniard who lived among the coastal Indians and roamed Texas between 1528 and 1536. Beginning with Cabeza de Vaca's 1542 published account, we know some of the names of Indian groups, and we also have direct information about their appearance and customs. In practical terms, though, it was not until the 1600s that European contact was intensive enough either to generate much information about Indian cultures in Texas or to influence them.

We do know that in this early contact period Texas was home to a wide variety of Indian groups with languages as divergent as English and Chinese. The groups followed different ways of life and sometimes competed with one another for territory and trade. After 1684, the French and Spanish also vied for influence in the region. Spanish friars established a network of mission communities for converting the Indians to Catholicism. These places became refuges where Native people would settle, either seasonally or continually, as they sought food and protection from their enemies. Some of these missions eventually became sites for further military and civil growth.

Of all the cultural elements introduced in the historic period, the horse had perhaps the most dramatic influence on Native Americans. Horses had become extinct in North America at the end of the Ice Age but lived on in Asia and Europe, where they were domesticated and bred into their modern forms. Conquistadors brought horses to the New World in 1541, and by 1650, some North American Indians had adopted horses that were rustled or escaped from the Spanish settlements. The Indians became superb riders, totally devoted to life on horseback. Texas was an abundant source of horses and good grazing, making the region all the more attractive to Indian migrants. The Caddo villages of East Texas became key posts for a far-reaching Indian horse trade, and horse people from the north—Apaches, Comanches, Kiowas—were drawn to the fine valley pastures of the Hill Country.

The horse had important effects on Indian life. It made occupation of the dry open grasslands a possibility. Whereas people on foot could not travel fast enough between scarce water holes to survive, mounted people could. Buffalo hunting became much more efficient when a single rider could chase and slay an animal from horseback. Horses were themselves another food source, at least during emergencies. Territorial defense, long-distance trade, and sudden attack and escape all became easier. A horse could also carry or pull much more than a dog could, while living on readily available grass instead of hunted meat. Portable tents could thus be bigger, and possessions of all kinds more numerous. Horses were so valued that they became a standard of wealth and a means of payment in marriage exchanges and lawsuits.

In all, life became richer for Indians who adopted the horse, and the classic image of the mounted Indian with a feathered warbonnet and tall tipi is a product of this process. Nevertheless, the times of the horse Indian were relatively brief and late. The Comanches arrived in Texas in the early to mid-1700s, after the Spanish and no more than four or five generations before the Anglos. Some historic Texas groups, such as farming peoples from the forested east, used horses but did not center their existence on them.

European materials such as iron and glass also became important during the contact era. For archaeologists, some of the common indicators of the historic period include glass trade beads and arrow points made from iron or glass instead of flint. Introduced firearms gave some Indian groups advantage over others and spurred intertribal fighting and migration. Smallpox and cholera (brought by the Europeans) had a greater effect than guns, however, killing thousands of Native individuals and entire societies and thus opening their areas for occupation by other Indians and non-Indians.

Even considering that Texas was always a dynamic human environment, the historic period was a time of great turmoil and rapid change. For better or worse, we think of this period as "the way Texas was," and we are most familiar with the Indian groups from this era. These groups are known by name and usually referred to as *tribes*, even though some were not tribally organized in a technical sense. More tribes lived in Texas during the historic period than in any other state.

Alabama

Name: The name is derived from a Choctaw term meaning "I clear the thicket."

Language: Alabama language, Muskhogean family; also Mobilian Jargon, an ancient intertribal trade language.

Origins: The Alabamas are traced to the Alabama River drainage in northeast Alabama around 1700, and possibly to Mississippi before that.

Time period in Texas: Began arriving via Louisiana about 1790; continuous occupants since.

Range: Big Thicket area of southeast Texas, mainly between the Neches and Trinity Rivers (Polk, Tyler, and San Jacinto Counties).

Population estimates: In 1809, the combined population of Alabamas and Coushattas within seventy miles of Nacogdoches totaled about 1,650.

Material life: The Alabamas depended on hunting, gathering, fishing, and fruit and vegetable gardening. After 1880, many became expert lumbermen. Trails and water routes connected hunting camps and settled villages that consisted of a central ceremonial square with cabins spread through the surrounding forest.

Social and political life: In Alabama, the tribe was part of the alliance of Muskhogean Indians called the Upper Creek Confederacy. The Alabamas have always been closely linked with the Coushattas. The tribe is composed of twelve (formerly thirteen) matrilineal clans connected through intermarriage, but it is also divided into two halves, the "Reds" and "Whites," for ceremonial purposes. Governance is by first and second chiefs who are elected for life and who, since the 1930s, work with an elected tribal council.

Beliefs: Tales about supernatural beings and animals explain the origin of the world and cultural practices such as agriculture. Pre-Christian rituals included the annual busk, or Green Corn Dance, and shamanic curing.

Modern location, numbers: The modern Polk County reservation, an enlarged version of the lands provided for the tribe in 1854, consists of nearly 4,594 acres. About five hundred enrolled Alabamas and Coushattas lived at this location in the 1990s, with a similar number living elsewhere.

Atakapan

Name: Atakapa means "eaters of men" in Choctaw.

Language: Atakapan, of undetermined origin.

Origins: Unknown, probably southeastern.

Time period in Texas: Prehistoric times to mid-1800s.

Range: Extreme southeast Texas and adjacent Louisiana; coast and bayous around the lower Trinity, Neches, and Sabine River basins.

Population estimates: Perhaps 3,500 in 1698, only 175 in Louisiana in 1805.

Material life: Hunting of deer, bear, and alligator; fishing; plant gathering; agriculture only for some inland groups. Trade with other tribes and with the French and the Spanish.

Social and political life: The Atakapans included several tribes: the Atakapas proper, the Bidais, Akokisas, Patiris, and Deodoses. Little is known of their domestic or social life.

Beliefs: Only faint evidence of Atakapan religion remains, including a creation myth that traces human origins to the ocean. Shamans administered plant cures, and some Atakapans used the "black drink" (yaupon holly tea), a stimulant and purgative used by Southeast Indians for ritual purification.

Modern location, numbers: The population dropped rapidly under European contact, mainly from disease, and the Atakapans were virtually extinct by the mid-1800s. There were nine known descendants in 1908.

Caddo

Name: Kadohadacho, a word meaning "real chief" or "real Caddo."

Language: Caddo (several dialects), Caddoan family.

Origins: The Mississippian southeast, moving through Oklahoma, Arkansas, and Louisiana in the late prehistoric period.

Time period in Texas: Late Archaic until 1859.

Range: Northeast Texas, along the Red River and upper Neches drainage. By the early 1840s, all Caddo groups had moved to the Brazos River to avoid Anglo colonization.

Population estimates: An 1829 Spanish estimate of three hundred families probably reflects a population already drastically reduced by disease and warfare.

Material life: The Caddos lived in substantial villages of large beehive-shaped houses built from poles and grass. They practiced advanced farming to produce corn, beans, and pumpkins, which was supplemented with some seasonal bear and buffalo hunting. The Caddos crafted distinctive baskets and pottery, built ceremonial mounds, and maintained trade networks for furs, guns, and horses.

Social and political life: The Caddos consisted of more than two dozen tribes organized in three confederacies: the Hasinais, Kadahadachos, and Natchitoches. Their society featured matrilineal clans linked by intermarriage. Religious and political authority was organized hierarchically, and each village had a hereditary chief priest called *xinesi;* a *caddi,* or hereditary civic headman; and *canahas,* or secondary headmen or village elders.

Beliefs: Worship, led by the chief priest, focused on a male supreme god, the *Caddi Ayo,* plus powerful spirits. Medicine men treated the sick. Rituals included harvest, late winter, and naming ceremonies.

Modern location, numbers: The Caddos were removed from Texas to Indian Territory (Oklahoma) in 1859, at which time they numbered about 1,050. Descendants continue to live in western Oklahoma, around Binger and Anadarko. There were 4,350 Caddos on the tribal rolls in 2002.

Cherokee

Name: The English term comes from *Tsalagi,* "Cave People" in Choctaw; Cherokees used the Choctaw name for themselves, and also *Ani-Yunwiya,* "Real People."

Language: Cherokee (originally three dialects), Iroquoian family.

Origins: The Cherokees are an ancient offshoot of the Iroquois of the northeastern United States, living in the southern Appalachians by 1540.

Time period in Texas: First known arrival in 1807, with significant migration after 1820; most expelled to Indian Territory (now Oklahoma) in 1839, with some remaining or returning to Texas.

Range: The Tennessee–North Carolina border region and adjacent areas in the 1700s; migrants to Texas settled in the northeast among the Caddo villages, mainly on the upper Sabine River and its tributaries.

Population estimates: An 1810 estimate notes 12,400 for the whole tribe; perhaps six hundred in Texas in 1830. In 1885, about nineteen thousand total were counted.

Material life: Long successful farmers and hunters, Cherokees had adopted log cabin dwellings and the raising of hogs, cattle, and sheep by the time they lived in Texas. They also adopted writing, cloth manufacture, slavery, and other traits considered "civilized" by Euro-Americans. During the Texas era, they had a distinct style of dress featuring frock coats, turbans, and sashes.

Social and political life: Elaborate social and political order with seven matrilineal clans linked by intermarriage. Towns, each with a council of elders, were the main settings of political action, linked through larger regional councils for alliance. Dual war and peace chiefs were appointed by an assembly to lead larger efforts.

Beliefs: Myths and rituals centered on the veneration of *totems*, the animals considered ancestors of human clans, to ensure continued prosperity. Manipulation of spiritual power for curing or witchcraft was practiced.

Modern location, numbers: The Cherokees in Oklahoma are organized as the Cherokee Nation, with their capital at Tahlequah and with 222,651 citizens in 2002. Another ten thousand Cherokees affiliate with the fifty-seven-thousand-acre Qualla Reservation in North Carolina. Unofficial as well as recognized claims of Cherokee ancestry have become very popular throughout the United States; in the 2000 federal census, 729,533 people identified themselves as part or all Cherokee.

Cheyenne

Name: English name from the Sioux name *Shai-ena*, "People of Alien Speech." The Cheyennes refer to themselves as *Tsitsitsas*, "People Alike" or "Our People."

Language: Cheyenne, Algonkian family.

Origins: Known as a farming tribe in Minnesota in 1680, the Cheyennes migrated south and west to the Missouri and Arkansas River valleys over the 1700s and 1800s, while abandoning farming for buffalo hunting from horseback. One branch, the Southern Cheyenne, rode the Southern Plains with Comanches and Kiowas during the 1800s. Throughout their history, they have been closely associated with the Arapaho tribe.

Time period in Texas: About 1820 to 1875.

Range: Great Plains, occasionally into Texas.

Population estimates: Estimated at three thousand in the 1830s; 2,055 counted in 1875.

Material life: The Cheyennes pursued the classic mobile buffalo-hunting culture of the plains, living in tipis and maintaining large horse herds.

Social and political life: Organization was in small nomadic bands, built around cores of relatives, which sometimes congregated to form larger units. People traced descent through both mother and father, like modern Americans, allowing for many different options in cooperating with relatives for hunting, camping, and warfare. A council of forty-four peace chiefs, each chosen for a ten-year term, decided civil matters. The Dog Soldiers, one of seven men's military societies, influenced policy in the closing days of Cheyenne independence.

Beliefs: Mythology referred to the time the people "lost the corn," that is, abandoned agriculture, as well as to the supernatural origins of the Council of Forty-Four. The Cheyennes had several major rituals, including the Massaum animal dance, the Sun Dance, and the renewal of the four sacred arrows that safeguarded tribal fortunes. Some reservation Cheyennes were among the early practitioners of the religion centered on use of peyote, a hallucinogenic cactus.

Modern location, numbers: About 11,400 Cheyennes and Arapahos were enrolled in Oklahoma in 2002. The former reservation land in Oklahoma includes the areas around Watonga and Clinton.

Coahuiltecan

Name: The general name was adopted by anthropologists from *Coahuilteco,* one of dozens of names for small bands recorded by the Spanish.

Language: Numerous dialects, proposed Coahuiltecan language and family.

Origins: Little is known of Coahuiltecan origins, beyond their presence in northern Mexico and South Texas in the early historic period and, presumably, the prehistoric.

Time period in Texas: From the prehistoric until about 1800, by which time the Coahuiltecans were largely absorbed into Hispanic society.

Range: South Texas plains and scrub, north into the margins of the Edwards Plateau and south into Coahuila, Nuevo León, and Tamaulipas.

Population estimates: The total Coahuiltecan population and the sizes of bands prior to colonization are difficult to assess. Estimates including the Mexican bands have ranged as high as eighty-six thousand to one hundred thousand people.

Material life: The Coahuiltecans were mobile hunters and gatherers, living on deer, javelinas, and rabbits; smaller animals; and scrub plant seeds and fruits. Food sources were often meager. They produced few goods and lived in small brush dwellings.

Social and political life: Not enough is known about the social or political organization of the Coahuiltecans. They lived in hundreds of small bands with flexible membership and with much sharing and equality among individuals. Some evidence points to patrilineal descent, a custom aiding the sharing of men's hunting knowledge from one generation to the next.

Beliefs: Little is known about Coahuiltecan myths or rituals. Shamanism and individual seeking of spirit power are presumed practices. Group feasting and dancing are known historically, notably during the summer prickly pear harvest. The Coahuiltecans were early ceremonial users of the hallucinogenic cactus peyote.

Modern location, numbers: During the colonial period, many Coahuiltecans were displaced from their traditional territories by advancing Spaniards and Apaches and were hence brought into the missions. Epidemics, regional warfare, and infant mortality took tolls on the population, and the survivors adopted Hispanic identities. Few Coahuiltecan ethnic unit names appear in documents after

1800. Nevertheless, people claiming Coahuiltecan descent still live throughout northern Mexico and South Texas.

Comanche

Name: The name *Comanche* comes into English from Spanish, though it is originally a Ute Indian name meaning "other." Comanches call themselves *Nʉmʉ* or *Nʉmʉnʉʉ*, "Our People."

Language: Comanche is a language of the Numic branch of the Uto-Aztecan family and is nearly identical to Shoshoni.

Origins: The Comanches are an offshoot of the Shoshoni Indians of Wyoming.

Time period in Texas: 1743 (first recorded observation) to 1875.

Range: Home territory after the mid- to late 1700s was the Plains and Hill Country of northwest and Central Texas, plus adjacent Oklahoma, with travels through neighboring states and Mexico. They were located on a reservation in Indian Territory (now Oklahoma) with the Kiowas and Kiowa-Apaches around 1875.

Population estimates: Eighteenth- and nineteenth-century estimates vary widely, from six to twenty thousand. A reservation census counted 1,382 in 1884.

Material life: The Comanches pursued the classic mobile buffalo-hunting culture of the plains, living in tipis and maintaining large horse herds. They had the greatest horse wealth of all the tribes and controlled much of the Southern Plains trade in goods, livestock, and captives during the early and mid-1800s.

Social and political life: Flexible, autonomous family-based bands gathered or separated, adjusting to changing opportunities. Large band groupings now referred to as divisions functioned like independent tribes. Major divisions included the Penatekas (Honey Eaters), Kotsotekas (Buffalo Eaters), Yamparikas (Root Eaters), Kwahadis (Antelopes), and Nokonis (Wanderers). There was no continuous overarching leadership or regular meeting of all Comanches, though division leaders could mobilize large groups for hunting, trade, or warfare.

Beliefs: Comanches conducted solitary vision quests to acquire supernatural power from animal spirits and human ghosts for health, war and hunting success, and curing. There were also some group ceremonies for sharing power. On the reservation, Comanches led the development of the peyote religion.

Modern location, numbers: The Comanche population reached a low of 1,171 in 1910. In 2000, the tribe numbered about eleven thousand people, half of whom live in the area of the former reservation around Lawton, Oklahoma, and the rest across the United States.

Coushatta

Name: Coushatta is a form of *Koasati,* which probably contains the Muskhogean elements for "cane," "reed," or "white cane."

Language: Koasati, Muskhogean family, though not nearly identical to the Alabama language as previously reported.

Origins: The Coushattas are traced to the Alabama River drainage in northeast Alabama around 1750.

Time period in Texas: Began arriving via Louisiana in the 1780s, continuous occupants since.

Range: Big Thicket area of southeast Texas, mainly between the Neches and Trinity Rivers (Polk, Tyler, and San Jacinto Counties).

Population estimates: In 1809, the combined population of Alabamas and Coushattas within seventy miles of Nacogdoches totaled about 1,650. In 1812, six hundred Coushattas were estimated along the Sabine River, and in 1850, an estimate of five hundred is given for the population of two villages on the Trinity River.

Material life: The Coushattas depended on hunting, gathering, fishing, and fruit and vegetable gardening. After 1880, many became expert lumbermen. Trails and water routes connected hunting camps and settled villages, which consisted of a central ceremonial square with cabins spread through the surrounding forest.

Social and political life: The Coushattas were originally members of the Upper Creek Confederacy. Social units and customs were similar to those of the Alabamas. In Texas, the Coushattas inhabited several villages, each with a local chief, in turn governed by a principal chief. Since 1859, when they moved onto the reservation originally established for the Alabamas, the Texas Coushattas have lived under the Alabama chiefs and tribal council.

Beliefs: Tales about supernatural beings and animals explain the origin of the world and cultural practices such as agriculture. Pre-Christian rituals included the annual busk, or Green Corn Dance, and shamanic curing.

Modern location, numbers: Most Texas Coushattas joined the Alabama Reservation in Polk County in 1859. A few remained at the site of a former Coushatta village in San Jacinto County until 1906 and then moved onto the reservation. The Polk County Coushattas are counted in the Alabama-Coushatta tribal population (893 in 1993). In 1990, there were 389 Coushattas living on the Koasati Reservation near Kinder, Louisiana.

Delaware

Name: From the river valley where they originally lived and named for the English governor Baron De La Warr; they called themselves *Lenni Lenape,* "Real Men."

Language: Delaware (multiple dialects), Algonkian family.

Origins: First known in the areas surrounding the Delaware River, including parts of present-day New York, New Jersey, Pennsylvania, and Delaware.

Time period in Texas: About 1820 to 1859.

Range: Once driven from their original lands by white settlement, the Delawares moved westward to establish villages in Ohio, Indiana, Illinois, Wisconsin, Ontario, Missouri, Kansas, Oklahoma, and Texas. In Texas, they inhabited the northeast, near the Red and Sabine Rivers. Most were expelled with the Cherokees in 1839, but some remained; these often served as scouts and ranged widely throughout Texas. In 1859, most of the last Texas Delawares were sent to Indian Territory (now Oklahoma) to live on a reservation with the Caddos and Wichitas.

Population estimates: Owing to their wide distribution, it is difficult to give dependable numbers for the Delawares. Nineteenth-century totals suggest perhaps three thousand altogether. An estimated seven hundred were in Texas in 1820.

Material life: The Delawares were woodland gardeners and hunters living in single-room bark lodges called *wigwams.* They made pottery, baskets, and dugout canoes.

Social and political life: Small villages along waterways, each with its own headmen, functioned as confederated but independent units. Munsee, Unami, and Unalachtigo were often recognized as Delaware subgroups in earlier descriptions, though the number and nature of subgroups are frequently debated. In each subgroup, relatives organized in ten to twelve patrilineal clans linked by intermarriage.

Beliefs: The turtle was the central character in their creation myth. Worship was directed at a supreme being and guardian spirits. Rituals were conducted in a lodge called the Big House, which represented the universe; twelve faces were carved in its supporting posts, representing messengers to the Creator. The main ceremony of thanksgiving and renewal lasted twelve days.

Modern location, numbers: Descendants of the Texas Delawares sent to Indian Territory reside among the Caddos and Wichitas in the vicinity of present Anadarko and Carnegie, Oklahoma. In 2002, the Oklahoma Indian Affairs Commission reported 1,304 Delawares. Other significant Delaware populations, totaling over eleven thousand, reside in eastern Oklahoma, Wisconsin, Kansas, and Ontario.

Jumano

Name: Jumano is the standardized form of a tribal name recorded by the Spanish in several versions, and it is of unknown origin.

Language: Jumano; earlier thought to belong to the Athapaskan or Uto-Aztecan families, but recently placed in Tanoan, a family associated with the eastern Pueblo Indians.

Origins: The Jumanos may have been descendants of the Jornado Mogollon, Puebloan Indians living along the Rio Grande in prehistoric times.

Time period in Texas: About 1500 to 1700.

Range: Lower central Texas and the Rio Grande near present Presidio, though also along trade routes throughout Texas, eastern New Mexico, and northern Mexico.

Population estimates: Spanish reports are usually inexact, or they pertain to small local groups, making overall estimates difficult. There were probably several thousand over the entire range.

Material life: People of this ethnic group apparently lived either as farmers in fixed river villages or as nomadic buffalo hunters and traders farther north. Dwellings were either permanent adobe houses with flat roofs or portable skin tents. Dogs were probably used to transport a rich variety of raw materials and luxury goods. The Jumanos adopted and spread horses early from Mexico but did not develop a major horse culture. The Spanish recorded Jumano use of clubs and wooden bows reinforced with horn or sinew; otherwise, little is known of their tools and weapons.

Social and political life: Each village and camp identified one or two *caciques,* or headmen; little else is known of Jumano organization.

Beliefs: Not known.

Modern location, numbers: The Jumanos fade from history around 1700, disrupted by invading Apaches and absorbed into surrounding populations, including the Apaches and Caddos.

Karankawa

Name: The name originally pertained to one subgroup; although of uncertain meaning, it possibly means "Dog Lovers."

Language: Karankawa, a little known language with no clear connection to others.

Origins: Archaeological remains labeled the Aransas Focus and Rockport Focus show populations ancestral to the Karankawas living in the same locations as early as the Archaic. Further origin points are uncertain.

Time period in Texas: Prehistoric period to about 1858.

Range: Gulf Coast between Galveston and Corpus Christi Bays. Most moved toward Mexico in the final days of the tribe.

Population estimates: Estimates for the population at the time of earliest European contact range between twenty-eight hundred and eight thousand. In 1828, one hundred families were estimated for two subgroups; only a few dozen people remained by 1843.

Material life: The Karankawas exploited coastal bays and marshes in dugout canoes, depending on fish, shellfish, turtles, and alligators. They also hunted inland for deer and bison. As nomadic hunters, they carried few possessions, though they made clay cooking pots lined with natural asphalt. Dwellings were round huts of willow framework covered with skins or mats.

Social and political life: Small nomadic bands led by headmen would dissolve into individual family units when food was scarce. The Karankawas included five major subgroups: the Carancaguases (Karankawas proper), Cocos, Cujanes, Coapites, and Copanes.

Beliefs: Religion may have centered on two deities who are now obscure, and probably other spirits and powers. Rituals included ceremonial cannibalism and *mitotes,* gatherings featuring dancing and consumption of the "black drink," a stimulant and purgative made from yaupon holly.

Modern location, numbers: The Karankawas avoided a fatal confrontation with the Spanish but suffered heavily from disease after early Spanish contacts. They fell quickly after the Anglo invasion of their area around 1820. They were considered extinct after a Texan attack on the last small remnant group in 1858.

Kickapoo

Name: From the self-name *Kiikaapoa,* "He Stands About."

Language: Kickapoo (Algonquin dialect), Algonkian family.

Origins: The Kickapoos are closely related to the Sauk and Fox tribes of the Great Lakes area. They are traced to lower Michigan in the 1640s, Wisconsin in the 1660s, and Illinois in the 1760s. During the 1800s, they formed separate groups in Kansas, Oklahoma, and Mexico (via Texas).

Time period in Texas: Around 1800 to present.

Range: In Texas, initially east of the Trinity River, later through central Texas and into Mexico, returning from there to the border area.

Population estimates: In 1825, twenty-two hundred were estimated at all locations. By the end of the nineteenth century, about four hundred were based in Mexico.

Material life: The Kickapoos alternated sedentary village life with hunting trips. They farmed corn, beans, and squash; they hunted deer, bison, and bear. They were known as excellent riflemen and had horses on the Southern Plains, although they did not convert to a nomadic horse society. Homes included winter structures of heavy frames covered in bark or mats, and oval summer lodges made from poles and reeds.

Social and political life: Relatives lived in extended families and were organized in eleven patrilineal clans, named for animals and nature elements, that were linked through intermarriage. People's names reflected their clan affiliations, for example, "Bush Growing from a Cliff" for a member of the Berry Clan. Traditional leaders included a hereditary chief and council of elders. Since the 1930s, these leaders have been supplemented with elected officials as required by Mexican and U.S. policy.

Beliefs: A rich body of myths features animal characters and the sons of a supreme being, one of whom is a creator figure. In Mexico, the Kickapoos have maintained a yearly calendar of traditional rituals. A feast and dance of the clans celebrated in Mexico around late January is the main group ceremony.

Modern location, numbers: El Nacimiento, Coahuila, and Eagle Pass, Texas, were home to a connected population of about five hundred in 2000. Other populations with some overlap to the Mexican and Texas groups are found in central Oklahoma near McCloud and Jones, and also around Horton, northeast Kansas.

Kiowa

Name: From self-name *Kaigwu,* "Principal People"; also *Kompabianta,* "People of the Large Tipi Flaps."

Language: Kiowa, Tanoan family.

Origins: Traced to the Yellowstone region of Montana and the Black Hills of South Dakota, though their Tanoan language shows a connection with Puebloan people found historically in New Mexico. One recent theory explains the Kiowas as a remnant of the Jumanos.

Time period in Texas: About 1790 to 1875.

Range: Southern Plains into northwest Texas, with journeys through Central and West Texas and northern Mexico. They were located on a reservation in Indian Territory (now Oklahoma) with the Kiowa-Apaches and Comanches around 1875.

Population estimates: Numbers prior to the reservation are not known—perhaps a few thousand. In 1875, there were 1,070.

Material life: The Kiowas pursued the classic mobile buffalo-hunting culture of the plains, living in tipis and maintaining large horse herds.

Social and political life: Extended families functioned as hunting bands. There were no hereditary clans, but people joined age grades and military societies. Wealthier and poorer people were distinguished in four classes. The tribe consisted of six subtribes, or bands, including the Kiowa-Apaches, each with a position on the camp circle when all convened. Councils selected civil chiefs and war leaders.

Beliefs: Myths described Sun Boy, a hero who bestowed sacred medicine bundles called the Ten Grandmothers. Veneration of the bundles was necessary for tribal well-being. Individuals sought guardian spirits on vision quests. The Sun Dance in June was the great annual tribal ritual. On the reservation, Kiowas became early practitioners of the peyote religion.

Modern location, numbers: The Oklahoma Indian Affairs Commission reported 11,200 Kiowas in 2002, many living in the former reservation area around Anadarko, Fort Cobb, Mountain View, and Carnegie, Oklahoma.

Kiowa-Apache

Name: So named in the late nineteenth century because of their Apache language and connection with the Kiowas. They usually call themselves simply "Apache" or *Naishan Dene,* "Our People."

Language: Apache (dialect), Athapaskan family.

Origins: Athapaskan-speaking peoples, including all those now called Apaches and Navajos, can be traced to northwest Canada and Alaska. The Kiowa-Apaches were a small group of Athapaskans that attached itself to the Kiowas. Some studies place this event in the early historic period, thereby linking the Kiowa-Apaches with the Lipans and other eastern Apaches.

Time period in Texas: About 1790 to 1875.

Range: Southern Plains into northwest Texas, with journeys through Central and West Texas and northern Mexico. They were located on a reservation in Indian Territory (now Oklahoma) with the Kiowas and Comanches around 1875.

Population estimates: Through the 1800s, about 300 to 350 people.

Material life: The Kiowa-Apaches pursued the classic mobile buffalo-hunting culture of the plains, living in tipis and maintaining large horse herds.

Social and political life: The Kiowa-Apaches formed a subtribe of the Kiowas. Although they kept their own language and some social customs, they took their place on the Kiowa camp circle and generally resembled their hosts. There were four Kiowa-Apache societies: one for boys, two for men, and one for older women.

Beliefs: The Kiowa-Apaches participated in the Kiowa Sun Dance, and individuals sought power from guardian spirits on vision quests.

Modern location, numbers: In 1910, after starvation and epidemics, the population dropped to 139. In 1966, the Kiowa-Apaches formed the Apache Tribe of Oklahoma, which enrolled two thousand people in 2002. They live around the Oklahoma towns of Apache, Boone, Fort Cobb, and Anadarko.

Lipan Apache

Name: "Apache" is a general Spanish term, probably from the Zuni word *apachu,* "enemy." "Lipan" is the Spanish adaptation of *Ipan'de,* apparently "Ipa's People"; Lipans called themselves *Naishan,* "Our Kind."

Language: Lipan (Apache dialect), Athapaskan family.

Origins: Athapaskan-speaking peoples, including all those now called Apaches and Navajos, can be traced to northwest Canada and Alaska. The Lipans emerged among the Apachean people who had migrated onto the Southern Plains before or during the early historic period.

Time period in Texas: From the early 1700s, when first recorded by the Spanish as a specific group (or earlier) until about 1875.

Range: Through much of Texas, gradually forced into New Mexico, South Texas, and Mexico by invading Comanches during the 1700s.

Population estimates: Perhaps eight thousand in the 1750s. An 1805 estimate counts 750 men, possibly three thousand for all individuals. After the 1850s, no more than a few hundred were counted.

Material life: The Lipans combined some corn gardening in Hill Country canyons with seminomadic hunting and gathering. They were early pioneers of plains horse culture, though not sharing in all the traits of later Southern Plains Indians like the Comanches and Cheyennes. Certain Southern Plains customs, such as use of the lance and smoke signaling, may be traceable to the Lipans. They normally lived in brush wickiups and sometimes used tipis.

Social and political life: Extended family bands led by headmen were the main form of organization. They probably had clans like other Apache groups, which were named for natural features in the landscape rather than animals.

Beliefs: Little direct evidence remains, but their beliefs are assumed to have resembled those of other Apache and Southern Plains peoples, centering on the control of supernatural power, vision questing, and shamanism.

Modern location, numbers: The Lipans were displaced first by the Comanches and then by European settlers. Individuals intermarried with other tribes or merged into Hispanic society in Texas and Mexico. In 1905, thirty-five remaining Lipans were identified, living among the Mescalero Apaches in New Mexico and the Tonkawas and Kiowa-Apaches in Oklahoma.

Shawnee

Name: From Algonkian term *shawanogi,* "Southerner."

Language: Shawnee (Algonquin dialect), Algonkian family.

Origins: Traced to the Ohio River valley in prehistoric times.

Time period in Texas: About 1820 to 1859.

Range: During the historic period, the Shawnees lived progressively in South Carolina, Georgia, Pennsylvania, Tennessee, Kentucky, Ohio, Missouri, and Kansas. Some of the Missouri Shawnees migrated into Texas via Arkansas, Oklahoma, and Louisiana. In Texas, they lived in the northeast, south of the Red River. Most were expelled with the Cherokees in 1839, but some remained; these often served as scouts and ranged widely throughout Texas. In 1859, most of the last Texas Shawnees were sent to Indian Territory (now Oklahoma).

Population estimates: Numbers range from one to two thousand for the entire tribe during the historic period. Estimates of three to six hundred Shawnee families in Texas in the 1820s are probably exaggerated. An 1851 report counts seventy Shawnees in Texas.

Material life: Woodlands pattern of corn, squash, and beans gardening plus hunting. Villages were substantial but abandoned for migratory winter hunting trips. In the east, the Shawnees also participated in the fur and salt trades.

Social and political life: The Shawnees had thirteen clans with animal totems, interlinked by marriage. The tribe was also divided into five units. Representatives of the five divisions met in a council house to make public policy and chose leaders.

Beliefs: Worship focus shifted in the 1800s from a male supreme being to a female creator figure called Our Grandmother. Various nature spirits were also worshipped. Rituals included the Green Corn or Bread thanksgiving dances conducted at the council grounds. The Shawnees also had sacred bundles and medicine men.

Modern location, numbers: Today Shawnees reside in three groups in Oklahoma: the Absentee tribe between Shawnee and Norman, and the Eastern and Loyal tribes in the northeast corner of the state. The population for the three tribes totaled about twelve thousand in the 1990s.

Tigua

Name: Spanish version of self-name.

Language: Tiwa, Tanoan family.

Origins: Pueblo villages of the upper Rio Grande in New Mexico: Taos, Picuris, Sandia, and Isleta. The Tiguas in Texas migrated from Isleta to the El Paso area along with the Spanish who retreated downriver during the Pueblo Revolt of 1680.

Time period in Texas: 1680 to present.

Range: Settled at Ysleta, near El Paso, and hunted over surrounding counties.

Population estimates: About 317 Tiguas came to Texas in the Spanish retreat. A 1750 census records five hundred Indians at their settlement; another in 1787 indicates 195 persons.

Material life: The Tiguas farmed corn and other crops, hunted deer and rabbits, and gathered desert plants. Their early dwellings were rectangular adobe apartment houses of the Pueblo type. During the 1800s, they made unpainted pottery that was used throughout the area.

Social and political life: Kin lines were originally traced through females, but the matriclan system has given way to Euro-American family patterns. Tigua tribal organization follows the Puebloan model, a native structure modified by the Spanish. Men of the tribe elect officials including a lieutenant governor, war captain, sheriff, captains, majordomos, and council members. The council in turn appoints the *cacique,* a religious leader for life, and a civil administrator called the governor.

Beliefs: Concepts of spiritual beings and powers have been blended with Catholicism. The Tiguas maintained a version of the Kachina Cult in Texas. The tribe also observes four yearly Catholic holy days, the most important for their patron St. Anthony on June 13, with traditional dancing and feasting.

Modern location, numbers: The Tigua settlement of Ysleta grew into a suburb of El Paso. A Tigua reservation in this community was established in the early 1970s, and in the 1990s, tribal lands were also purchased in nearby Socorro and near Valentine, Texas. Tribal rolls in 2002 listed 1,254 members of one-eighth blood quantum or greater.

Tonkawa

Name: From a Waco name, *Tonkaweya,* "They All Stay Together." The Tonkawas called themselves *Titskanwatitch.*

Language: Tonkawa, Tonkawan family.

Origins: Whether the Tonkawas lived in Central Texas in prehistoric times or migrated there from the north in the 1600s has been a matter of debate. In either case, they are not clearly connected to other historically known populations.

Time period in Texas: Uncertain; known to the Spanish by 1740.

Range: Central Texas Hill Country and toward the coast.

Population estimates: Spanish and Anglo estimates, often reporting only families or warriors, suggest a total population of perhaps six hundred to fifteen hundred during the late 1700s and early 1800s.

Material life: The Tonkawas lived on bison, deer, smaller game, fish, and plant foods such as prickly pear and pecans. They dwelled in small tipis made from bison skin, replaced by brush tipis or huts once the buffalo were killed off in their area. They adopted the horse early but did not develop the kind of full horse culture seen among the Comanches and Kiowas. They were good traders, exchanging hides and meat for Caddo pottery. They made their own baskets, mats, and bark cloth.

Social and political life: The Tonkawas embraced a number of bands of varying sizes, some of which probably had non-Tonkawan backgrounds. Normally there was a headman for each band; an overall chief was chosen to help join the bands in the face of continuous contact with invading tribes and non-Indians. People lived together as members of matrilineal clans that were linked through intermarriage.

Beliefs: Little is known, apart from some evidence of shamanism, gods, ghost beliefs, and ritual cannibalism.

Modern location, numbers: The Tonkawas became impoverished as their lands were taken over by Apaches, Comanches, and non-Indians. In the mid-1800s, they often served as scouts against the more western tribes. In 1859, about three hundred were removed from Texas to Indian Territory (Oklahoma), where three years later they were decimated in a revenge attack by Delawares and Shawnees. In 1885, at the establishment of a Tonkawa reservation around present Tonkawa and Oakland, Oklahoma, only 92 persons survived. The Tonkawa Tribe of Oklahoma was organized in 1938 and counted 404 members in 2002.

Wichita

Name: Origin uncertain; possibly from *wits,* Wichita for "man," or *wia chitoh,* Choctaw for "big arbor." They call themselves *Kitikitish,* "Raccoon Eyes," a reference to face painting or tattooing.

Lanugage: Wichita, Caddoan family.

Origins: People ancestral to the Wichitas moved onto the central plains from the Southeast Woodlands during the Archaic. In the late prehistoric and early historic period, they occupied the Arkansas River and neighboring drainages in Kansas and Oklahoma. Some may also have pioneered the upper Canadian River in the Texas panhandle in these times.

Time period in Texas: Mid-1700s to 1859, not counting possible panhandle occupants.

Range: After the mid-1700s they lived around the Wichita Mountains in southwest Oklahoma and along Texas rivers, between and including the Red and Colorado.

Population estimates: Estimates across two or more villages count thirty-two hundred in 1778 and twenty-eight hundred in 1809; these numbers are thought to reflect large reductions by disease and warfare.

Material life: The Wichitas lived in fixed, fortified villages, farming corn, melons, tobacco, and other crops. They also undertook seasonal buffalo hunting trips. Their villages were centers for trade where Plains Indians brought hides to exchange for Wichita produce. They also manufactured goods for white settlements farther east. Their homes were large beehive-shaped pole-and-thatch lodges.

Social and political life: The Wichita Confederacy included the Wichitas proper, Taovayas, Tawakonis, Wacos, Kichais (a late addition with a different Caddoan language), and other groups. Villages, each headed by a chief and subchief, were the largest political units. Households were organized around women, but individuals traced descent through both parents as modern Americans do.

Beliefs: The Wichitas believed in a supreme creator being and other gods associated with the stars. Secret religious societies paid homage to these beings in dances. Shamanism was also practiced.

Modern location, numbers: The Wichitas were removed from Texas to Indian Territory (Oklahoma) in 1859. About four hundred were reported at the time of removal. Modern descendants live around Anadarko and Gracemont, Oklahoma. There were 2,150 members of the Wichita and Affiliated tribes (including Waco, Tawakoni, and Keechi) in 2002.

❷

EAST TEXAS

E ast Texas has a distinctive geographic character, quite different from other sections of the state. The tall hardwood and pine forests broken by prairie and farmland, a warm humid climate, and the patterns of human history tie the eastern Lone Star State to other sections of the Deep South. However, the Indian and non-Indian societies of the region also have a southeastern flavor. The Native Americans who were indigenous in the prehistoric and early historic periods, as well as those who migrated in during the 1800s, represented cultures tied to the southeast.

In most cases, the Anglos and African Americans who arrived in numbers after the 1820s came from the Gulf states. Even today, the small towns north and east of Houston and their inhabitants very closely resemble those in, say, Mississippi. The colorful Franco-American cultures of the Creoles and Cajuns associated with Louisiana have also spilled across the Texas side of the state line. Environmentally, socially, and culturally, that line has always been an uncertain boundary.

The Native heritage of the region is best understood then as an extension of the lifeways of the Woodland Indians. This classification has long been used by scholars for Indians of the eastern seaboard, distinguishing these Indians from the horse people of the Plains or the Southwest desert dwellers. Woodlands Indians typically hunted deer and gardened corn, beans, and squash in forest clearings.

A further distinction is often drawn between Northeast and Southeast Woodlands cultures. In the south, Indians were prone to settle in relatively large, often fortified, towns along rivers, hence the tribal name "Creek" given by the English. They had linguistic and ceremonial traits in common with one another but different from the forest dwellers of the north. Some of the Southeastern groups were descended from or influenced by the prehistoric Mississippian people, who achieved complex societies approaching those of the Mayas and Aztecs of ancient Mexico; their spectacular mounds (platforms for chiefdom buildings and burials), elaborate grave goods, and religious artifacts are found through much of the South.

The historical experience of Indians in East Texas unfolded amid conflict. Most of the historical tribes were refugees from Anglo expansion in Georgia, Alabama, Mississippi, Arkansas, and Louisiana. The Spanish welcomed these Indians as settlers in Texas, hoping they would serve as a buffer against further Anglo expansion toward Mexico. But the deep woods and bayous were inviting to adventurers and outlaws, whose presence among the Indians soon led the way for traders and then planters. When the cotton economy crept into Texas, the Indians had to confront what they had earlier avoided.

Among the dominant groups in the late prehistoric and early historic periods were the Caddos. The Caddos came to Texas from the east, though prior to the big push of Anglo settlement. Their tribal name embraces a number of related populations living in fixed agricultural villages of grass lodges with names such as Hasinais, Kadahadacho, Anadarko, and Neches. The Caddo villages formed a confederacy for trade and mutual protection, the members of which were referred to as *tejas,* "friends." This term was then extended to the non-Indian friends of the Caddos who came to trade with them. It eventually became the basis for the region name Texas.

The Caddos had moved into Texas from adjoining parts of Arkansas and Louisiana in the late historic period. Over time, the various Texas Caddo settlements relocated again, more than once, in response to intrusions by other Indians and whites. Through all, they served as important headquarters for regional trade, and they maintained at least some vestiges of the rich ceremonial life of the prehistoric Southeast, including mounds, authoritative priests, and political leaders.

The Wichitas, who were linguistic relatives of the Caddos, also farmed and lived in grass houses. They relocated to Texas from Kansas, reaching Oklahoma in 1719 and crossing the Red River after the 1750s; several Wichita subgroups lived in permanent villages along Texas rivers, including the Wichitas proper, the Wacos, Tawakonis, and Kichais. Both the Caddos and Wichitas ventured annually onto the high plains to hunt buffalo, living in skin tipis when they went. Mainly, however, the plains horse Indians came to them, bringing hides to the villages to trade for corn and pumpkins. Although the Wichitas settled well onto the Rolling Plains, they are discussed here because the Indian village at modern Waco is treated as an East Texas site.

The Alabamas and Coushattas are two closely related peoples who migrated west from the Coosa River basin in northern Alabama to Louisiana, and then into Texas after about 1790. They were able hunters and traders who preserved, in addition to their tribal tongues, an ancient trade language called Mobilian Jargon, which was used among the various Southeastern tribes for intertribal communication. In the early decades of the 1800s, they had several villages connected by a trail system around Polk and Tyler Counties. They were aloof but not antagonistic to Anglo Texans: They refused to side with Mexico in the fight for Texas independence; they aided Texicans fleeing before Santa Anna's army in 1836; and some even manned riverboats for the Confederate Navy. In gratitude for their early loyalties, Sam Houston helped establish the Alabama-Coushatta Reservation in 1854, and he admonished the Indians to never let the sun set with a white man on their land—advice they tended to follow. Alabama and Coushatta people still reside on this reserve in Polk County and maintain their languages, basketry, and other cultural traditions.

Chances are, if a Texan today claims Indian descent, he or she affiliates with the Cherokees. The presence of this well-known tribe in Texas was relatively brief, but of lasting influence. At the dawn of the historic period, the Cherokees were native to the mountains of eastern Tennessee, western North Carolina, and northern Georgia. They had a comparatively complex social order, with agriculturally based towns managed by councils of elders but linked regionally via trade and warfare alliances.

By the late 1600s, the Cherokees had continuous contact with white settlers, and they gradually formed many of the institutions then considered marks of higher civilization: schools, writing, a newspaper, cloth clothing, plows, a constitutional government with bicameral representation, and slavery. Still, the relentless pressures of Anglo settlement prompted many Cherokees to seek a more peaceful life to the west. They entered Texas by 1807, and by 1830, four hundred Cherokees lived in several towns between the Sabine and Neches Rivers.

Most of those who remained in their Appalachian homeland were removed between 1838 and 1839 in the infamous forced march to Indian Territory (now eastern Oklahoma) called the Trail of Tears, in which perhaps four thousand perished. But in East Texas, the Cherokees found uncertain relations with the Spanish, Mexicans, and Anglos; in addition, the Comanches roamed to their west, thus limiting any more migration. Despite the efforts of Sam Houston, who was adopted and married into the tribe as a young adventurer, the Texas Cherokees were denied title to the land they occupied. In 1839, they were driven to Indian Territory by military force; their leader Duwali and over one hundred of his followers were killed in the defense of their range near present-day Tyler, Texas.

Other Indian migrants entered East Texas during this era of upheaval. Kickapoos came in from the Great Lakes area, Delawares and Shawnees from the northeast via the Midwest. A small branch of the Creek or Muskogee Indians called the Pakana Muskogees accompanied their ancient neighbors, the Alabama and Coushattas, and settled in Polk County.

Perhaps long before any of the groups mentioned, the Atakapans lived in southeast Texas along the rivers emptying into the Gulf. Some scholars believe that the Atakapan language clearly linked them to other tribes of the ancient Southeast, but others are not so sure. We know relatively little about these coastal plain dwellers because they died off from diseases introduced by Europeans before there was much steady contact.

In seeking traces of the Indian past in East Texas, we proceed literally down the trail, for the most notable kind of feature in this region is the "trace," or trail, blazed by Native travelers. A robust system of traces crisscrossed the area forests and linked Indian villages when white pioneers arrived. These routes were the forerunners of Spanish and Anglo roads and town sites. Thanks to a few diligent historians, the courses of many of these trails, and the locations of the Indian villages they connected, are still determinable. This information is especially valuable in a region that does not have many natural landmarks of the dramatic kind found in the open, dry reaches of West Texas. In East Texas, few stark single hills mark the horizon; springs are plentiful (so any particular one is less critical to human survival); and the heavy forestation contributes to an entirely different visual environment.

Indians' cultures were disrupted early in this part of Texas, a situation that might make the Native sense of geography more remote to us. This disconnect, however, is partly offset by the sheer intensity of Anglo settlement activity in the region and the reliance of these pioneers on Indian trails, which has led to a good deal of preservation of knowledge about Indian locales and travel routes.

THE LAY OF THE LAND

East Texas is underlain by four geologic bands corresponding to the Upper Cretaceous, old and later Tertiary, and the Pleistocene, with the bands progressively newer toward the coast. On the surface are two broad physiographic zones: the Blackland Belt running along the boundary with the High Plains on the western side of the East Texas region, and a much wider swath of Gulf Coastal Plain toward the ocean. The rich dark soils of the blacklands host prairie

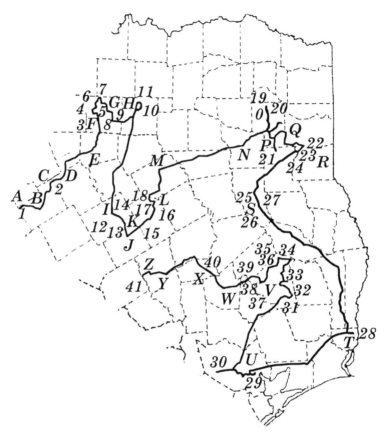

East Texas

Sites

1. Indian Gap
2. Johnson Peak
3. Isaac Parker Cabin
4. Trinity Park
5. Cold Springs
6. Marine Creek
7. Blue Mound
8. Village Creek
9. Johnson Creek
10. White Rock Creek
11. Moss Park
12. Waco Springs
13. Tehuacana Creek
14. Torrey's Trading Post
15. Big Hill
16. Old Fort Parker
17. Comanche Crossing of the Navasota River
18. Tehuacana Hills
19. Cherokee Trace
20. Indian Rock
21. Cherokee Village
22. Nadaco Village
23. Cherokee Bayou
24. Bowles Spring
25. Delaware Indian Village
26. Caddoan Mounds
27. Cherokee Trace Angelina River Crossing
28. Atakapan Campsite
29. Peggy Lake
30. Bear Creek, Buffalo Bayou
31. Colita's Village
32. Old Alabama-Coushatta Campground
33. Alabama-Coushatta Reservation
34. Peach Tree Village
35. Coushatta Trace
36. Long Tom's Trace
37. Long King's Village
38. Indian Hill
39. Kickapoo Trace
40. Poole's Creek
41. Ranchería Grande

Towns and Cities

A. Indian Gap
B. Hamilton
C. Hico
D. Iredell
E. Cleburne
F. Fort Worth
G. Arlington
H. Dallas
I. Waco
J. Marlin
K. Coit
L. Mexia
M. Corsicana
N. Tyler
O. Gilmer
P. Kilgore
Q. Easton
R. Tatum
S. Alto
T. Orange
U. Houston
V. Livingston
W. Huntsville
X. Madisonville
Y. Wheelock
Z. Hearne

vegetation made up of bluestem, grama, and buffalo grass. Eastward on the Gulf Coastal Plain, woodlands take over.

Adjacent to the blacklands is a post oak belt that includes post and blackjack oaks as well as hickory, somewhat like the Cross Timbers of the Rolling Plains (see chapter 5). Yet further east, covering the largest portion of the region, are the piney woods. Stands of short-leaf pine mixed with oaks are found in the more northerly piney woods; in the south, shortleaf pine mixes with longleaf and loblolly pine in deep, majestic stands. These are the general patterns only. Irregular prairies and savannahs are found in the forest zones, and the woodlands run out onto the Blackland Belt along stream channels. Beech, cypress, gum, tupelo, and palmetto are some other species that are common or dominant in certain areas.

Rainfall patterns help determine the plant life. Annual rainfall graduates from about thirty-four inches on the blackland prairies to as much as fifty-eight inches in the extreme southeast corner of the state. Compare these rates to the eight to twelve inches characteristic of the western tip of Texas. The Texas towns that are on record officially for the most rain in a year and a single day are both in East Texas: Clarksville, Red River County, 109 inches in 1873; Thrall, Williamson County, 38 inches in 1921 (respectively). Nevertheless, the annual rainfall in East Texas is distributed about equally across summer and winter.

Apart from high rainfall, weather extremes are rare in the east, with the exception that late summer hurricanes periodically ravage the upper Texas coast. The storm that landed at Galveston on September 8, 1900, was the deadliest natural disaster in the nation's history, killing perhaps eight thousand people. It is most important to note that throughout East Texas rainfall is sufficient to support farming without special water pumping, irrigation, and conservation techniques—so the area was very attractive to Native peoples who supplemented their hunting with cultivated vegetables.

In particular, the rivers of the region—the Trinity, Neches, Angelina, Sabine, and Red—supported the same kind of village farming lifestyle that Indians enjoyed in the Deep South; they also made migration from Alabama and Louisiana more enticing. Other water features such as sloughs, oxbow lakes, and cypress swamps harbored fish and game and thus attracted Indian settlements at their edges. Modern stream damming formed most of the large lakes evident today; however, Indian sites were sometimes drowned in the process. The Brookes Saline at the junction of Saline Creek and the Neches River, seven miles west of Bullard in Smith County, was a famous Indian salt source and the nexus of many trails; it is now under the waters of Lake Palestine. The site of the Upper Village of the Coushattas (Battise Village), dating to 1830, lies hidden beneath Lake Livingston.

Parts of the Blackland Belt are still like a perfect picture of prairie America, with rolling terrain, waving grass, and porch-wrapped Victorian frame houses. Caddo National Grassland in Fannin County offers a glimpse of the original landscape. Elsewhere in the blacklands, native plant and animal life have been pushed to the property lines by years of intensive cultivation—first cotton and later a variety of other crops.

Lumbering caused similar changes to the forests: The heyday of the timber industry coincided with the building of railroads, as East Texas provided the railroad crossties. After World War II, wood pulp production was the driving force behind the clearcutting of thousands of forest acres. Oil wildcatters also cleared swaths to reach well sites, while saltwater and petroleum pollution from the oil wells fouled area streams and lakes. Fortunately, large stands of pine, hardwoods, and palmetto have been maintained or revived at Angelina, Davy Crockett, Sabine, and Sam Houston national forests, and in the Big Thicket National Preserve, so that all may gain some sense of what Indians came across.

In the piney woods and hardwoods, the atmosphere is dark and mysterious. Texans raised in the big sky country of the open plains feel claustrophobic among the tall pines. Pioneers referred to the tangled Big Thicket growth as "tight-eye," a very descriptive name in English, though really a corruption of an Indian word. According to a local folk saying, the brush is so dense that rattlesnakes have to crawl through it backward. Here steep-banked rivers run slow, deep, and muddy, loaded with toothsome gars and snapping turtles.

River bottoms hold overflow water in sloughs and swamps apart from the main river channels. We have watched alligators surfacing like submarines through the duckweed in McCordell Lake, just off busy U.S. 59 near Goodrich. Cougars, bears, and red wolves once abounded in the region, as did turkeys, deer, and bobcats, who along with coyotes and wild razorback hogs are common today.

In the old days, the density and monotony of the forests required a different sense of navigation than would be required on the plains. Without long vistas, it was the pathways themselves, rather than landmarks, that oriented travel. Still, the region comprised certain distinctive geographic features. The Great Raft was a tangle of driftwood some thirty miles long that dammed the Red River in Louisiana to form Caddo Lake, which extends into Texas. Another interesting feature is the Kisatchie Wold (Cuesta, Escarpment), a line of low hills running between the Mississippi River and the Rio Grande, formed by erosion from a continuous ridge of sandstone. In East Texas, the wold runs nearly east-west, parallel to the coast. The steeper slope of the ridge faces inland. This feature deflects streams flowing toward the Gulf, a phenomenon that can be seen on a map in the eastward loops formed along the Trinity and Neches Rivers. As on the high plains, an escarpment of this kind offered sheltered microenvironments that would have attracted game and Native hunters. It was also a continuous landmark in an otherwise uniform terrain.

In traveling the East Texas region today, we find excellent roads that sometimes follow the old trails but other times cut across ancient pathways. In either case, car travel provides an adequate feel for the landscape and allows access to much of the area's Indian past.

EXPLORING EAST TEXAS

The East Texas tour begins at **Indian Gap,** in the far western corner of Hamilton County, east of Brownwood and west of Hamilton, at the intersection of FM 218 and FM 1702.

Indian Gap, in the low hills of far west Hamilton County, was used by the Comanches for passage to and from the white settlements during the early and mid-1800s.

> To reach **Johnson Peak** from **Indian Gap,** take FM 218 east about 17.6 miles to the DH 36 intersection at Hamilton; take U.S. 36 east about .5 miles to the U.S. 281 intersection; take U.S. 281 north about 20.7 miles to the SH 6 intersection at Hico; take SH 6 east about 9.2 miles to the FM 1238 intersection at Iredell; take FM 1238 south about 1.9 miles, to the second curve in the road; **Johnson Peak** is the prominent point almost straight ahead to the southeast, 1.1 miles away.

In 1858, Kiowas and Comanches made a raid near this landmark that resulted in the death of Peter Johnson. The mesa became known as Johnson's and then **Johnson Peak;** it is also called Meridian Peak. Johnson's son was captured in the raid but escaped from the Indians a short time later.

> To reach the **Isaac Parker cabin** from **Johnson Peak,** return north on FM 1238 about 2.8 miles, through Iredell and across the North Bosque River, to the FM 927 intersection; take FM 927 north about 8.9 miles to the SH 144 intersection; take SH 144 north about 14.3 miles to the U.S. 67 intersection at Glen Rose; take U.S. 67 east about 23.6 miles to the SH 174 intersection at Cleburne; take SH 174 north about 15.7 miles to the IH 35W intersection; take IH 35W north about 13.3 miles to the intersection of IH 30; take IH 30 west about 2.6 miles to the University Drive exit; take University Drive south about 0.8 miles; the **Isaac Parker cabin** is visible on the right.

The **Isaac Parker cabin** is located in Fort Worth's Forest Park. In 1862, after Cynthia Ann Parker was recaptured from the Comanches, she was taken to the Fort Worth area to live with her Anglo kinsmen (see the **Fort Parker** entry, pp. 49–50). When she was brought in, schools closed and crowds showed up to view her on Fort Worth's courthouse square. She spent some of her last years living in the cabin of her uncle Isaac Parker, who had initially identified her when she was recaptured. The cabin was located near Birdville when Cynthia Ann lived in it.

To reach **Trinity Park** from the **Isaac Parker cabin,** return north on University Drive to the IH 30 intersection; continue north on University about 0.2 miles and turn right on Trinity Park Drive, which meanders through the park.

According to an old newspaper account, an Indian village was located at the site of Fort Worth's **Trinity Park** around the time of the Civil War. The tribe may have been one the Caddoan groups, but its identity remains uncertain; perhaps a number of tribes were represented, for the area was a refuge for displaced and recombined Native groups. A local story tells of the time an Indian from the village entered the home of one Mrs. Cope and forced her to cook a supply of food for him. The small bands of Indians lingering around the Trinity Forks were considered treacherous by the Anglos, even though they were openly friendly. By the 1860s, the villager tribes were desperately seeking some way of continuing to survive in the face of massive displacement.

To view the vicinity of **Cold Springs** from **Trinity Park,** continue on Trinity Park Drive to the Crestline intersection; take Crestline west about 0.3 miles to the University Drive intersection; take University Drive north (right) about 0.1 miles to the West Lancaster Avenue intersection; take West Lancaster Avenue east (right) about 1.4 miles, to the Henderson Street intersection; take Henderson Street north (left) about 0.6 miles to the Belknap Street/SPUR 347 intersection; take Belknap Street/SPUR 347 east (right) about 0.5 miles to the BR 287/North Main Street intersection; take BR 287/North Main Street north (left) about 0.2 miles, to the Trinity River Bridge; the precise location of **Cold Springs** is somewhere downstream (right) along the riverbank, although it is still debated by the locals.

The foot of the Main Street bridge at the junction of the Clear Fork and West Fork of the Trinity River is the approximate location of **Cold Springs.** Originally a Comanche meeting place, the site appeared perfectly suited for a military camp to explorers Middleton Tate Johnson and U.S. Army Brevet Major Ripley A. Arnold (see the "Johnson Creek" entry, p. 44). On June 6, 1849, they founded Camp Worth, soon Fort Worth, named in honor of their Mexican

War commander General William J. Worth. In short order, Indians visited the post. Arnold wrote:

> About 100 Indians of the different wild tribes are now visiting me. They brought down and delivered up some thirty-six horses which they had taken from the Wichitas—horses stolen within the last year from citizens. Three Wichita chiefs are here, and promise everything for the future. All is peace and quiet on this frontier. (Quoted in Baker and Cage 1962, p. 11)

To reach **Marine Creek** from **Cold Springs,** continue north on North Main Street about 2.4 miles, just past the Exchange Avenue intersection; at this point is a crossing of **Marine Creek.** To view **Marine Creek** in a more pastoral setting, continue north on North Main Street about 1 mile to the West Long Street intersection; take West Long Street west (left) about 0.4 miles, to **Marine Creek.**

The Trinity River tributary **Marine Creek** that now winds through the Fort Worth metropolitan area was often used as an avenue of approach for Indians moving southeast toward the Trinity Forks from the Rolling Plains. In the unsettled days before the Civil War, Caddos took up residence along the route; their lodges were on view along Bluff Street. These Indians sometimes came visiting the Anglo citizens of Fort Worth, but the townspeople remained fearful of attack. According to an old settler's recollection, Indians killed a cow three miles north of town in the Marine Creek brakes one Sunday morning in March 1869. In June 1871, Indians rode along the creek for several miles, killing five to six hundred Anglo horses. In 1876, Indians again killed horses at area ranches while traveling along Marine Creek. The raiding Indians were likely Kiowas or Comanches straying from the Oklahoma reservation.

To reach **Blue Mound** from **Marine Creek,** return east on West Long Street to the BR 287/North Main Street intersection; take North Main Street north (left) about 1.4 miles to the SH 156/Terminal Road intersection; take SH 156/Terminal Road north about 3.5 miles to the

Western Center Road intersection; **Blue Mound** is on the southwest corner of this intersection.

The notable hill called **Blue Mound** stands 864 feet above sea level on the divide between the West and Elm Forks of the Trinity River. It would have marked the way for travelers coming from the Rolling Plains toward Indian villages and camps in what is now the Dallas–Fort Worth metroplex area. Anglo settlers near the landmark understandably fell victim to Indian attacks, especially once troops had been diverted from the Texas frontier to serve in the Civil War.

According to an interview with an old settler conducted during the Great Depression, Comanches captured three hundred settlers' horses at Blue Mound on July 1, 1869. Leaving their own mounts behind as they fled, the Indians drove the stolen stock along nearby Silver Creek and right past a camp meeting in progress. The worshippers joined irate stock herders in pursuing the Indians westward into the next county. One Indian was killed in the pursuit, but the horses were apparently not recovered. A year earlier, two young Anglo boys who had been left to tend some remaining cows and horses after an Indian raid were surprised at Blue Mound and chased away by three Indians.

The metroplex bedroom community of Blue Mound some six miles south of the hill takes its name from the landmark, but it flourished only after the 1930s, when the Globe Laboratories and Aircraft Company were founded.

Just 4.6 miles east of Blue Mound lies the town of **Watauga.** The town is on a site thought to have been a prior Cherokee settlement place. Its name has been explained as a Cherokee word meaning "village of many springs." Since there is no longer an identifiable Indian feature to focus on at this location, our route bypasses the town.

To reach **Village Creek** from **Blue Mound,** take Western Center Road east about 1.7 miles to the IH 35W intersection; take IH 35W south about 1.3 miles to the Loop 820 intersection; take Loop 820 east and

> then south about 13.1 miles to the U.S. 80/180/East Lancaster Avenue intersection; take East Lancaster east about 2.9 miles to the crossing of **Village Creek.**

Village Creek was the site of several Indian settlements that were destroyed by Texas militiamen in 1841. A rural Anglo community sprung up on the creek in the later 1800s but has since been absorbed into the Dallas–Fort Worth metropolitan area. Most of the battle area is now under Lake Arlington, but one can get a glimpse of the creek bed habitat above or below the lake.

Texan attempts to find and raid Indian settlements along the upper Trinity River began in 1838 but were unsuccessful until May 1841. That month, sixty-nine Republic of Texas volunteers under General Edward H. Tarrant made their way through the east and west Cross Timbers and came upon fresh signs of Indian traffic. They found two deserted villages on high ground (probably the heights east of present Mountain Creek Lake) and destroyed these with their axes, fearing that if they burned the lodges, Indians ahead would be warned away by the smoke. On May 24, the militia then came upon an inhabited village along present Village Creek and quickly overran it in a surprise horse charge. They moved northward a few miles and hit a second village in the same manner. Farther along were more villages of increasing density. The Indian defenses came alive and stalled the advance of the Texans, many of whom were by then on foot in the thickets of the creek bed. Some Indian prisoners revealed that at least five hundred warriors lay ahead, so Tarrant withdrew. At least a dozen Indians had been killed, and much stolen property was recovered.

In the strict sense, the Texans were routed, but their attack was enough to begin forcing the tribes away from their upper Trinity River homelands for good. When Tarrant returned to the site in July with a force of four hundred men, he found the villages freshly abandoned. The Indians never returned here. Although some accounts reported the Indians at Village Creek to be Comanches, it is obvious from other records that this was mainly a refuge for farming tribes. In fact, some records mention huts and acres of cornfields. Cherokees, Caddos, Wacos, Kickapoos, and Tonkawas were all probably among the inhabitants. The Battle of Village Creek was a key event in opening the way for white settlement in the Fort Worth area. Tarrant's name lives on in the county designation, while the city and county of Denton are named after John B. Denton, Tarrant's aide who was felled by an Indian musket ball while approaching the main grouping of lodges—the only Texan fatality.

> To reach **Johnson Creek** from **Village Creek,** continue east on East Lancaster Avenue about 4.1 miles to the Cooper Street intersection; take Cooper Street south (right) about 2.1 miles to the SPUR 303 intersection; continue south on Cooper Street about 0.1 miles to the Arkansas Lane intersection; take Arkansas Lane east (left) about 0.1 miles to Vandergriff Park and **Johnson Creek.**

Around the headwaters of **Johnson Creek** (formerly called Mill Creek), at the springs once called Fossil Springs or Marrow Bone Springs, there was an old Indian camping place and a boulder upon which the Natives ground corn. Attracted by the good water and occasional presence of Indians and encouraged by the signing of an Indian treaty in 1843, some unknown adventurers set up a trading post at the site in 1845. Mexican War veteran Colonel Middleton Tate Johnson served in a Texas Ranger company headquartered at the springs, and he obtained a land grant nearby around 1847. Johnson soon became a prosperous cotton planter, and the settlement around his home became known as Johnson's Station. He renamed the springs Mary Le Bone Springs, which must have sounded more poetic or civilized to him. In June 1849, Johnson and U.S. Army Brevet Major Ripley A. Arnold located an army outpost at Cold Springs some fourteen miles to the west, first called Camp Worth, then Fort Worth (see the "Cold Springs" entry, pp. 40–41). Johnson's Station was bypassed when the railroad between Dallas and Fort Worth was built and when the population shifted north a few miles toward the tracks, giving rise to present Arlington. Johnson died in 1866 and was honored with the naming of Johnson County, Texas.

To reach **White Rock Creek** from **Johnson Creek,** return to Cooper Street; take Cooper Street south (left) about 1.9 miles to the IH 20 intersection; take IH 20 east about 14.1 miles to the U.S. 67 intersection; take U.S. 67 north about 9.3 miles to the IH 30 intersection; take IH 30 east about 3.8 miles to the Grand Avenue exit; take Grand Avenue north about 3.1 miles, to the Winstead intersection; take Winstead west (left) about 0.6 miles to White Rock Road and **Gateway Park** (known locally as White Rock Park).

The Trinity River and its tributaries at present-day Dallas attracted Indians of most or all the regional tribes at one time or another, including Cherokees, Shawnees, and Delawares. Contemporary Comanche leaders have indicated that their ancestors were familiar with the Dallas area, which they called Three Rivers. They recognized the Trinity's three major forks; however, whether the Spanish name (and thus English name) refers to the three branches is less clear.

Two major Indian traces forded the Trinity near present downtown, bringing the trading post that was the forerunner of the city. Until a few years ago, an interesting reminder of this heritage could be found in **Gateway Park** east of **White Rock Creek:** a long, horizontally trunked pecan that locals called "the rainbow tree," which is thought to have been an Indian marker tree. Comanches staked over saplings so they would grow pointing in the direction of a water-hole campsite. The trees were selected to stand out on ridges or near the edge of overgrowth to guide riders from trails toward springs hidden from their view.

Horizontal tree trunks occur naturally as well, especially among live oaks and mesquites, with their unusual growth habits. Although we know of no prostrate trees of undisputable Indian origin, there are at least a few trees still growing in Texas that have long been considered to be marker trees by local landowners and the State Forest Service (and there are others that also might qualify with further study). Comanche leaders visited the tree at Gateway Park in 1997 and proclaimed it a living monument to their historic presence in Texas. Unfortunately, the pecan, then estimated to be between 150

The *"rainbow tree"* at Moss Park, Dallas, a possible Indian marker. Photo by Ginnie Siena Bivona

and 300 years old, was soon after pronounced dead and removed. A wrought iron fence erected by the parks department now protects its saplings.

To reach **Moss Park** from **White Rock Creek,** return to Grand Avenue (which becomes Gaston Parkway, to the left); take Gaston Parkway north about 2.0 miles to the Buckner Boulevard intersection; take Buckner Boulevard northwest (left) about 2.2 miles to the Northwest Highway intersection; take Northwest Highway west about 3.0 miles to the Greenville Avenue intersection; take Greenville Avenue north (right) about 1.3 miles to the Walnut Hill intersection; continue north on Greenville Avenue about 0.4 miles and enter **Moss Park** on the right.

Stop at **Harry S. Moss Park** to view another possible Indian marker tree. Follow the sidewalks from the parking lot to find this a fine old Texas ash growing horizontally right along the ground, pointing the way to the waters of White Rock Creek. Like the tree formerly found at Gateway Park, it is also affectionately known by area residents as "the rainbow tree." Further study is needed to determine if this tree is old enough to be a real Indian marker, but in the meantime, it is fun to imagine that it could have been one.

To reach **Waco Springs** from **Moss Park,** return to Greenville Avenue and Walnut Hill; take Walnut Hill west about 0.6 miles to the U.S. 75/Central Expressway intersection; take U.S. 75/Central Expressway south about 7.6 miles to the IH 35E intersection; take IH 35E south about 97 miles, to the Waco Drive exit; take Waco Drive southwest about 2.4 miles, across the Brazos River bridge; take the FIRST LEFT past the bridge and continue about 0.3 miles; at this point, the street crosses the drainage of **Waco Springs;** park nearby to view the springs.

Waco Springs was once the site of a Waco Indian settlement, giving the modern city its name. Like the other branches of the Wichita people, the Wacos were a farming tribe that grew corn, pumpkins, beans, and melons around long-term settlements composed of beehive-shaped houses made from heavy pole frameworks covered with bluestem grass thatching. Thomas Duke, an American observer at the site in 1824, counted sixty of these large dwellings, housing several hundred people. The Wacos had four hundred of the surrounding acres under cultivation. They built earthworks all around the town for protection, as well as five underground forts within these walls where people could hide under attack. Despite these fortifications, Cherokee Indians moved into the area around 1830 and drove the Wacos away.

The springs rise a short distance away and join the Brazos River on its west bank. They would have provided a purer source of water for the village than would the river. Duke reported that the spring water was ice cold, enough that he only needed brandy and sugar to make a good cocktail. Other Wichita groups, the Taovayas and Tawakonis (of which the Wacos were an offshoot), had similar settlements farther up and down the Brazos during the early 1800s. This site must be typical of the places that the Wichitas chose to farm. Once they left this site, it continued to attract traders and settlers from other Indian and non-Indian groups.

To reach **Tehuacana Creek** from **Waco Springs,** return northeast on Waco Drive to IH 35; take IH 35 south about 0.2 miles to the SH 6 intersection; take SH 6 east about 3.2 miles; at about this point, highway signs will mark the crossing of **Tehuacana Creek.**

The bank of **Tehuacana Creek** was the site of a series of historic meetings between Indian representatives and Texas officials during the 1840s. The location was apparently an old council ground for the tribes that was activated by the Anglos for trade and negotiation—the Torrey brothers established their trading posts nearby (see next entry). On March 28, 1843, Tonkawas, Lipan Apaches, Wacos, Tawakonis, Caddos, and Delawares convened for a peace council. In April of the following year, a similar parlay was called by President Sam Houston; yet another meeting in October 1844 brought together some Penateka Comanches, Lipans, Wichitas, Caddos, Delawares, Shawnees, and Cherokees to sign a peace and commerce treaty. Two more councils followed in the fall of 1845 to involve other portions of some of the tribes.

To reach **Torrey's Trading Post** from **Tehuacana Creek,** continue east on SH 6 about 2.3 miles, to the Harrison Road intersection; take Harrison Road north about 1 mile to Trading Post Road; take Trading Post Road north about 1.5 miles; at this point, the site of **Torrey's Trading Post** will be visible to the east, on the bluffs north of Trader's Creek.

Travelers in this part of Texas today might be hard-pressed to imagine the kind of waterways and woodlands necessary to support beavers and otters, but in the early 1800s, even the far west edge of East Texas was rich in furbearers and an important source for the international fur trade. Less difficult to imagine here would be an abundance of deer; in fact, deerskins were also a major commodity in the early 1800s. The opportunity to obtain Indian-harvested pelts in exchange for manufactured cloth and metal items attracted enterprising Anglos to the frontier.

The Torrey brothers—John, David, and Thomas—were merchandisers of Connecticut Yankee stock specializing in the Indian trade. Their business was centered in Houston, but in the 1840s, they established a number of outposts to the west that more or less defined the line of settlement. At this site on the hill, in a grove of post oaks, was the second Torrey post built in this area. **Torrey's Trading Post No. 2** was a compound of a half-dozen log houses, one for pelts, another for trade goods, and the others as living quarters.

In 1848, another Connecticut trader, George Barnard, purchased this post and moved the business to Waco the following year. The Torrey posts were essentially the first banks in the region, with each trading house acting like a bank branch. Aside from their commercial contributions, the Torreys were important players in Texas Indian policy. It was no accident that **Torrey's Trading Post No. 2** was located just four miles from the old Indian council grounds on **Tehuacana Creek** (see previous entry). Their posts were meeting places for official Indian–white negotiations, and they made westward Anglo settlement more practical. The Torreys sometimes recovered captives and stolen horses from their Indian customers. John went on to establish some of the earliest mills and factories in the state, and he survived until 1893 in San Antonio. David opened a trading camp in Big Bend but was killed there by Apaches on Christmas Day, 1849. Thomas had died of disease in 1843 while scouting a new post location.

To reach **Big Hill** from **Torrey's Trading Post,** return to SH 6; take SH 6 east about 2.5 miles to the FM 164 intersection; take FM 164 east about 13.9 miles to the FM 339 intersection at Midway; take FM 339 south about 4.1 miles, to the intersection of FM 2489; take FM 2489 south and east about 3.5 miles, to **Big Hill.**

The **Big Hill** locality was named for an elevation on the blackland prairie that served Indians as a lookout point. An Anglo farming settlement grew here in the 1880s but was slowly abandoned after World War II.

To reach **Fort Parker** from **Big Hill,** take FM 2489 east about 9 miles to the SH 164 intersection at Groesbeck; take SH 164 east 3 blocks to the SH 14 intersection; take SH 14 north about 4.3 miles to the Park Road 35 intersection on the west (left) side of the road; take Park Road 35 west about 1.6 miles to **Fort Parker.**

At **Old Fort Parker State Historic Site,** visitors can view a replica of Fort Parker, a private fort consisting of cabins and a stockade built by the Parker family of settlers and their friends in

1834 or 1835. Fort Parker was not an Indian location except in the sense that it was built far enough west to prompt an attack by hundreds of Comanches and tribal allies; thus, it indicates Native notions of territory at the time. The May 19, 1836, attack set in motion the most famous personal saga in Texas Indian–white relations, for in this episode, Cynthia Ann Parker was captured at the age of about nine and taken into the Comanche tribe.

Parker became the wife of Chief Peta Nocona and mother of famed Comanche leader Quanah Parker. In his own personhood, Quanah embodied the tensions and resolutions of cultural conflict. He gained prominence as a resistance leader, then as a savvy reservation chief and businessman. He was the main spokesman for the tribe when he died in 1911.

Though recaptured and returned to her Anglo kin in 1860, Cynthia Ann never adjusted to white life again. She died heartbroken around 1871. Quanah had her reburied in Oklahoma, and mother and son now lie next to one another at Fort Sill, Oklahoma (see chapter 5).

To reach the **Comanche Crossing of the Navasota** from **Fort Parker,** return to SH 14; take SH 14 north about 8.3 miles to the U.S. 84 intersection at Mexia; take U.S. 84 west about 10 miles to the crossing of the Navasota River.

Local tradition records that the site of the U.S. 84 bridge was the favored **Comanche Crossing of the Navasota River.** It is easy to imagine Indians crossing the old ford on the fateful day that Fort Parker was attacked (see previous entry).

To reach **Tehuacana Hills** from **Comanche Crossing of the Navasota,** return east on U.S. 84 to the SH 14 intersection at Mexia; take SH 14 north about 0.1 miles to the SH 171 intersection; take SH 171 north about 5.4 miles to the crest of the **Tehuacana Hills.**

The modern community and the hills rising just west of it have the same name, **Tehuacana,** the Spanish rendition of Tawakoni; these Wichita Indians are said to have had a village in the hills in the early 1800s.

To reach **Cherokee Trace** from **Tehuacana Hills,** return to the SH
14 intersection at Mexia; take SH 14 north about 17.1 miles to the IH
45 intersection at Richland; take IH 45 north about 12.1 miles to the
U.S. 31 intersection at Corsicana; take U.S. 31 east about 62 miles to
the Loop 323 intersection at Tyler; take Loop 323 north and east about
6.4 miles to the U.S. 271 intersection; take U.S. 271 north about 37.1
miles to the SH 154 intersection at Gilmer; take SH 154 west (left) for
5 blocks to Montgomery Street; take Montgomery north (right) for 6
blocks; turn right again and go 1 short block; turn left—the next 4.6
miles of this road follow the old **Cherokee Trace.**

Here is a living remnant of the **Cherokee Trace,** an important migration and trade route linking the Nacogdoches area to
the Cherokee settlement at White River, Arkansas. The trail ran
north-south some miles west and roughly parallel to present U.S.
259. Indian trailblazers cut away trees and shrubs and matted down
lighter vegetation by dragging buffalo hides behind a horse over
the pathway. They marked fords and springs along the way, and
they are believed to have planted roses and honeysuckle as route
markers.

As the pressure of white settlement grew in East Texas, the trace
became an element in the Cherokees' undoing: Not only did it allow
thousands of Anglo immigrants to move in, but the Cherokees who
were expelled from Texas in 1839 were sent away on this very path.
Sam Houston and Davy Crockett were among the Anglo travelers of
the trace. Many of the earliest non-Indian settlers lived right along
the trail, a practice that gradually gave rise to villages on the route,
such as the now-vanished communities of Forest Hill northwest of
Gilmer, Lowe's Chapel in central Cherokee County, and Lilly in
southwest Camp County.

To reach **Indian Rock** from the **Cherokee Trace,** return to SH 154 at
Gilmer; take SH 154 east about 5 miles, past the FM 1650 intersection
on the right (south) side of the road; at this point, the highway passes
through **Indian Rock.**

Prior to World War II, the community of **Indian Rock** was a
thriving village of 150 people with a post office, mills, shops, and

schools. It was founded at the site of an Indian grindstone. The rock, about thirty feet in diameter, shows depressions used by the Cherokees and their predecessors for grinding corn.

To reach **Cherokee Village** from **Indian Rock,** return west on SH 154 to the U.S. 271 intersection at Gilmer; take U.S. 271 south about 16.1 miles to the SH 135 intersection; take SH 135 south about 12.1 miles to the SH 259 intersection at Kilgore; take SH 259 south about 8.3 miles, past the FM 850 intersection, to the crossing of Caney Creek; this was the site of **Cherokee Village.**

Maps from the 1830s locate a **Cherokee Village** at this location; however, there is no longer any trace of the settlement.

To reach **Nadaco Village** from **Cherokee Village,** return north on SH 259 about 11 miles to the SH 349 intersection at Kilgore; take SH 349 east about 10 miles to the intersection of SH 149; take SH 149 south and east about 1.7 miles, to the intersection of FM 2906; take FM 2906 east about 3 miles; from this point, less than 1 mile to the north (left), lies the site of **Nadaco Village,** on the bank of the Sabine River.

Nadaco, or Anadarko, roughly "place of sweet honey," was a Caddoan town name. The town was located at this spot around 1800. Anadarko, Oklahoma, where many Caddos were resettled after the 1850s, continues this name.

To reach **Cherokee Bayou** from **Nadaco Village,** return to SH 149 by heading south (right) from FM 2906 on any side road for about 1.2 miles; take SH 149 east a short distance to the dam on Cherokee Lake; the creek spilling from this dam is **Cherokee Bayou.**

Cherokee Bayou takes its name from an Indian town. In this vicinity, as many as seven villages along the creeks feeding the Sabine River housed Cherokee Indians around 1830. The Cherokee population in Texas peaked around this time at about four hundred, as the Mexican government encouraged them to settle here and become an obstacle to Anglo expansion.

To reach **Bowles Spring** from **Cherokee Bayou,** continue southeast on SH 149 about 6.5 miles to the SH 43 intersection at Tatum; take

SH 43 south about 18.9 miles to the U.S. 79 intersection at Henderson; take U.S. 79 south about 23.4 miles to the FM 110 intersection at New Summerfield; take FM 110 south about 13.2 miles to the U.S. 84 intersection; take U.S. 84 west about 0.9 miles to the U.S. 69 intersection at Rusk; take U.S. 69 south about 8.3 miles to the crossing of Bowles Creek; **Bowles Spring** is along the creek 0.8 miles to the southwest.

At **Bowles Spring,** the Cherokee leader Bowles (Chief Bowl, The Bowl, Duwali) signed a treaty in 1837 with Sam Houston that assigned lands along the Angelina River to Bowles's Cherokee followers. The treaty was not ratified by the Republic of Texas legislature, however, and the treaty negotiation was thus followed by orders from President Mirabeau Lamar for the Cherokees to leave Texas. In the armed resistance that resulted, Bowles and many of his people were killed.

To reach **Delaware Indian Village** from **Bowles Spring,** continue on U.S. 69 south about 3.4 miles to the SH 21 intersection at Alto; take SH 21 southwest about 1 mile; a **Delaware Indian Village** was once located near this point.

Relative latecomers to East Texas, the Delawares set up residence near the villages of other tribes during the 1830s and 1840s. A **Delaware Indian Village** near this point on SH 21 suggests how later Indian migrants were attracted to the same environments pioneered by earlier ones. This village was also close to Caddo settlements (see the next entry).

To reach **Caddoan Mounds** from **Delaware Indian Village,** continue south on SH 21 about 5 miles; **Caddoan Mounds State Historic Site** will be on the northwest (right) side of the road.

The **Caddoan Mounds,** formerly called Mound Prairie and currently known to scientists as the George C. Davis site, has been a human destination since deep in prehistory. Archaeologists have uncovered evidence of Paleo-Indian and Archaic activity here. The site is most notable, though, as the farthest southwest extension of late prehistoric Caddo ceremonial culture. Three large earthen mounds, two that supported civic buildings and one that contained burials, plus ample sign of domestic life indicate that a substantial village was in place here by around A.D. 900 and inhabited for five centuries. The town was the center of a large corn-farming operation and the destination for trail-bound traders from as far away as the Appalachians.

After 1300, the site was abandoned as Caddoan society decentralized and ceased mound building. Indians returned to the area, however: a village of the Neches tribe of Caddos stood nearby around 1700. The Spanish built a mission to serve the Neches, and their San Antonio Road passed here as well.

Visitors to the **State Historic Site** can see a replica early Caddo dwelling and interpretive center, and they can take a self-guided walking tour (about 0.75 miles). For current information on park hours and admission charges, call (936) 858-3218.

To reach **Cherokee Trace Angelina River Crossing** from **Caddoan Mounds,** return north on SH 21 about 6.2 miles to the U.S. 69 intersection at Alto; take U.S. 69 north about 0.2 miles to the FM 851 intersection; take FM 851 north about 10.4 miles to the FM 343 intersection; take FM 343 east about 2.9 miles to the crossing of the Angelina River; this is the **Cherokee Trace Crossing.**

This crossing was chosen by the Cherokee Indians when blazing the Cherokee Trace (see entry p. 51). The **Cherokee Trace Angelina River Crossing** became a well-known landmark for Anglo travelers. In the 1840s, David Rusk established a ferry service at the site, after which it became known as David Rusk Ferry. In 1850, Rusk's successor in the ferry business, H. G. Hatchett, opened an inn here and renamed the crossing after himself.

To reach **Atakapan Campsite** from the **Cherokee Trace Angelina River Crossing** return to U.S. 69 at Alto; take U.S. 69 south about 54.7 miles to the SH 63 intersection at Zavalla; take SH 63 south about 31.2 miles to the U.S. 190 intersection at Jasper; take U.S. 190 east about 1.6 miles to the U.S. 96 intersection; take U.S. 96 south about 34.5 miles, through Kirbyville and to the SH 62 intersection at Buna; take SH 62 south about 25.2 miles to the IH 10 intersection; take IH 10 east about 4.5 miles, to the 16th Street exit at Orange; take 16th

Street south (right) about 1.4 miles to the Park Avenue intersection; take Park Avenue east (left) four blocks, to 12th Street; take 12th Street south (right) six blocks to the Green Avenue intersection; take Green Avenue east (left) seven blocks to the 5th Street intersection; take 5th Street south (right) two blocks to the Front Street intersection; take Front Street east a short distance, and enter Ochiltree-Inman Park on the south (right) side of the road.

Remaining traces of the Atakapan Indians are hard to come by, since diseases introduced by the Europeans destroyed their society by the early 1800s. The banks of the lower Sabine River at Ochiltree-Inman Park in Orange are known historically as the location of an **Atakapan Campsite.** In fact, middens—mounds of discarded shells from continuous gathering of shellfish for food—found in the vicinity are thought to have been left by the Atakapans.

To reach **Peggy Lake** from the **Atakapan Campsite,** return to IH 10; take IH 10 west about 102.6 miles to the Loop 610 intersection on the east side of Houston; take Loop 610 south about 4.5 miles to the SPUR 225 intersection; take SPUR 225 east about 10.6 miles to the SH 134 intersection; take SH 134 north about 2.0 miles to the SH 1836 intersection; take SH 1836 about 1.2 miles to the San Jacinto Monument; walk to the base of the monument and look southeast to view Peggy Lake.

Known Indian campsites right in the Houston metroplex area are scarce. The open flat lands here were not considered hospitable places for setting up camp; the Comanche word for open prairie actually translates as "without people." Still, there is some record of Indian activity at a few places. The Akokisas, a branch of the Atakapan people, frequented the area according to one early Spanish account, and archaeologists have found artifacts showing prehistoric Indian occupations. **Peggy Lake** has yielded abundant evidence of prehistoric Indian camp life along the coastal estuaries. The Indians set up camps here centered on the harvesting of clams. Shells found among the archaeological remains, including large shell middens or refuse heaps, suggest that Indian people feasted on clams at Peggy Lake during May through July.

The prehistoric shell fishers also hunted the adjacent grasslands, marshes, and creek bed woods for deer, bison, small mammals, turtles, and snakes. The bones of these creatures are found along with the clam shells, as are arrow and dart points of stone and bone, as well as fragments of incised pottery, that is, pottery decorated by scratching lines and patterns in the clay while still wet. Large long-term settlements were the rule around **Peggy Lake** until about 1400, after which smaller seasonal camps seem to have been the norm. The later, more seasonal prehistoric visitors would have moved to inland base camps during cold weather. This pattern is similar to one the historic Atakapas and Karankawas would have employed.

> To reach **Bear Creek** from **Peggy Lake,** return to SPUR 225; take SPUR 225 west about 12.2 miles to the Loop 610 intersection; take Loop 610 west about 1.5 miles to the IH 45 intersection; take IH 45 north about 8.5 miles to the IH 10 intersection; take IH 10 west about 16.6 miles to the SH 6 intersection; take SH 6 north about 2.7 miles to the crossing of **Bear Creek.**

> To reach **Buffalo Bayou** from **Bear Creek,** return on SH 6 to the IH 10 intersection; continue south on SH 6 about 1.1 miles, to the crossing of **Buffalo Bayou.**

The network of creeks running through the Addicks and Barker Reservoir areas, including **Bear Creek** and **Buffalo Bayou,** can be considered the home turf of Atakapan Indians, including the Akokisas and Bidais branches. The Akokisas were described by the French officer Simars de Bellisle in the early 1700s as hunters, fishers, and gatherers who made large permanent camps in the winter while roaming in smaller groups during the summer. Direct evidence of an exact campsite for these historic Indians is lacking because white observers did not come into the area until a relatively late time. But prehistoric Indian camps found throughout the area, some dating to more than two thousand years ago, show how the historic Indians were likely to have lived.

Camps were set up right along the creek floodplains. They were occupied seasonally, as people moved toward and away from the coast in search of food. At **Bear Creek** and **Buffalo Bayou,** the people had a varied diet, with deer and a variety of turtles as the main foods, but also bison, antelope, badger, raccoon, possum, and rabbit. Archaeological remains have also included several human burials.

The reservoir area remained sparsely settled until the late 1900s, when land speculators enticed midwestern farmers to migrate there. Homesteads and roads, rice farms, and beef and dairy cattle operations marked the land. But the heirs of non-Indian settlers were forced off their lands in the 1940s as property was condemned to make way for a system of basins providing flood control for the city of Houston. The dam to create Barker Reservoir was finished in 1946, and Addicks Dam in 1948. The area then reverted to a state more like that encountered by Native inhabitants, as seen today.

To reach **Colita's Village** from **Buffalo Bayou,** return on SH 6 to the IH 10 intersection; take IH 10 east about 11.5 miles to the Loop 610 intersection; take Loop 610 north and then east about 8.6 miles to the U.S. 59 intersection; take U.S. 59 north about 26.3 miles to the FM 787 intersection; take FM 787 east about 17.8 miles to the FM 2610 intersection; take FM 2610 north about 6.3 miles; at this point, the site of **Colita's Village** is about 0.5 miles west (left), inside the bend of the Trinity River.

In this dramatic bend of the Trinity River lay the **Lower Coushatta Village.** The bend was named Shirt-Tail Bend by the old steamboat operators after they saw the long deerskin blouses of the Coushatta men living here. During the 1830s, this village was under the leadership of **Colita** (Kalita, Coleto, Colluta), one of the most celebrated East Texas Indian chiefs. He was born in the mid-1700s in northern Alabama and rose to prominence as the village chief at this site. Around 1838, he succeeded Long King (see entry p. 63) as principal chief of the Texas Coushattas. Colita was instrumental in maintaining peaceful relations between area tribes and the whites: In the 1836 Runaway Scrape, he supervised Indian efforts to aid settlers fleeing east from Santa Anna's advancing army, and he became legendary for an incident in which he personally helped some of these refugees in a dangerous crossing of the river. He died on July 7, 1852, while on a hunting trip at an age of perhaps one hundred. His passing was noted with sorrow in newspapers of the day.

To reach the **Old Alabama-Coushatta Campground** from **Colita's Village,** continue north on FM 2610 about 1.7 miles to the SH 146 intersection; take SH 146 north about 2.2 miles to the FM 943 intersection on the east (right) side of the road; take FM 943 east about 12.8 miles, to the FM 1276 intersection; take FM 1276 north, through Dallardsville, about 9.8 miles, and look for a parking lot for trail heads into the Big Sandy Unit of Big Thicket National Preserve; from this point, the **Old Alabama-Coushatta Campground** is about 1 mile to the north and can be approached along Big Sandy Creek.

Just below the southern boundary of the Alabama-Coushatta Reservation, at the junction of Big Sandy and Bear Creeks in the Big Sandy Unit of the Big Thicket National Preserve, is the **Old Alabama-Coushatta Campground,** a level area remembered as a favorite camping place of Alabama and Coushatta Indians in earlier times. Notes made by Stephen Austin for preparing a Texas map in 1827 show an abandoned Alabama village at this spot. It may have originally been a destination for Alabama and Coushatta travelers coming to hunt in the Big Thicket from farther east. This area was also the terminus of an eighteen-mile trail called the Campground Trace, which connected the campground to Long King's Village southwest of present Livingston (see **Long King's Village** entry, p. 63). It is perhaps no accident that the modern campground that was developed to support reservation tourism lies only a short distance north in the same floodplain.

To reach the **Alabama-Coushatta Indian Reservation** from the **Old Alabama-Coushatta Campground,** continue north on FM 1276 about 3 miles, to the U.S. 190 intersection; take U.S. 190 east about

4.8 miles to **Indian Village,** entrance on the south (right) side of the road.

Land for an Alabama reservation was purchased by the state of Texas in 1854 and occupied by some five hundred Alabamas in the winter of 1854 to 1855. It has been the tribe's home ever since. Grateful for the Indians' willingness not to side with Mexico in the war for Texas independence, Sam Houston influenced the effort that initially bought about 1,110 acres. At this point, both the Alabamas and Coushattas had been forced from their former village sites by white land claims and were living scattered throughout the woods on the brink of destitution. Several efforts to create a Coushatta reservation during the same period failed, so in 1859, most Coushattas were allowed to settle on the Alabama tract. In 1928, the property was expanded with an additional 3,071 acres and the enlarged reserve named the **Alabama-Coushatta Reservation.**

The main north-south road through the modern reservation corresponds to an old trail called the Alabama Trace. This trail was the major route between Alabama settlements in the early decades of the 1800s, and it once ran from the Spanish colonial San Antonio Road east of Nacogdoches, through Peach Tree Village (see the next entry) and the present location, on to Colita's Village (see p. 57) on the Trinity River. On the reservation grounds is the Presbyterian church that has been a community cornerstone since missionaries came among the tribes in 1881.

Nearby is the reservation graveyard, where seashells and also eyeglasses, coffee cups, and other favored possessions of the deceased are left on top of the graves; this poignant custom of decorating the graves is a Southeastern continuation of ancient Indian and African burial practices. The level area south and west of the church was originally the central ground of the village, used for dancing and playing *kopchi,* a Southeastern version of lacrosse in which players carried small netted sticks in each hand for passing a ball of stuffed deerhide. For these games and for certain ceremonial obligations, the population of the entire village was divided into two sides, the "reds" and the "whites."

Visitors will notice the distribution of reservation houses, spread around the forest in clusters here and there, linked by roads and footpaths; this pattern continues the arrangements typical of the eighteenth-century Alabama and Coushatta villages. Some of the home sites also have multiple buildings—newer houses built in front of older ones—which is a continuation of the old Indian practice of keeping separate dwellings for summer and winter. Since the 1960s, the reservation has been the focus of tourism development. The reservation is open to tourists from March through November. Camping is also available. Visitors can enjoy the cultural exhibits and craft shop (the Alabama-Coushattas are most famous for their pine needle and split cane basketry), as well as train and swamp buggy tours of the Big Thicket.

To reach **Peach Tree Village** from the **Alabama-Coushatta Indian Reservation,** return west on U.S. 190 about 2.6 miles to the FM 2500 intersection; take FM 2500 north about 6.2 miles to the FM 942 intersection; take FM 942 east about 8.2 miles to the FM 1745 intersection; take FM 1745 east about 7 miles to the U.S. 287 intersection at Chester; continue straight across U.S. 287 onto SH 2097 and proceed about 1.6 miles to **Peach Tree Village.**

Unlike the many other Alabama and Coushatta villages that stood in the forests of this area during the early and mid-1800s, **Peach Tree Village** lives on as an Anglo community that, though tiny, is recognized on modern maps. This village sitting atop the Kisatchie Wold was originally a thriving town of Alabama Indians who occupied the location before 1830. Fruit trees planted by the Indians supposedly gave rise to the town name, though the Alabamas also referred to it as Flea Village. Peach Tree was on the Coushatta Trace and also at the northern end of Long King's Trace. During the 1836 Runaway Scrape, the Alabamas gave shelter to Anglo refugees from the Mexican army at this village, showing a white cloth to indicate their friendly intentions. A few miles east, two other Alabama villages existed during the period: Fenced-in Village and Cane Island Village.

Grave decorated in traditional manner, Alabama-Coushatta Reservation. Photo by Daniel J. Gelo

To reach the **Coushatta Trace** from **Peach Tree Village,** return to U.S. 287; take U.S. 287 north (west) about 14.4 miles to the U.S. 59 intersection at Corrigan; take U.S. 59 south about 5.3 miles to the FM 350 intersection at Moscow; take FM 350 west—from this point, the next 10.4 miles of paved road plus an additional 1.3 miles of improved road to the community of Colita follow the **Coushatta Trace.**

Sweeping from east to west across northern Polk County is the old **Coushatta Trace,** corresponding to this section of FM 350. By the 1830s, the Coushattas blazed this trail to connect the Sabine and Colorado River basins, allowing communication and trade across a large part of the region. Before long, the trace was also an avenue for smugglers working between Mexico and Louisiana. The Spanish authorities had to post Coushatta scouts to monitor the traffic and report on illicit activity. The Coushatta Trace follows the Kisatchie Wold escarpment (see the earlier section, Lay of the Land, p. 38).

To reach **Long Tom's Trace** from **Coushatta Trace,** continue southward on FM 350; the section of road south of Colita follows **Long Tom's Trace.**

Long Tom's Trace is roughly followed by modern FM 350. Little is known about Long Tom except that he was an early-nineteenth-century leader of the Coushattas, probably comparable to Colita in his earlier career (see earlier entry, pp. 57–58). The trace and also the stream that passes along its upper reach, both named for Long Tom, indicate that his followers had settled in this area. This trail connected to the Coushatta Trace that ran east-west, farther to the north, and to Colita's and Long King's villages to the south. Somewhere along the trail, in the valley of Long King Creek, a momentous 1839 battle took place between the Coushattas and raiding Comanches. The Comanches were soundly repelled. According to contemporary Coushattas interviewed by Gelo, the defenders won by using the forest to their advantage—the mounted Comanches found it difficult to fight in the thick brush.

Indian Hill. Photo by Wayne J. Pate

To reach **Long King's Village** from **Long Tom's Trace,** continue southward on FM 350 to the U.S. 190 intersection; take U.S. 190 east about 1.2 miles to the U.S. 59 intersection at Livingston; take U.S. 59 south about 2 miles to the FM 1988 intersection; take FM 1988 west about 2.4 miles to the crossing of Tempe Creek; the site of **Long King's Village** is east (left) of the crossing.

Long King's Village was located here along Tempe Creek in the middle of three nineteenth-century Coushatta villages. It was the home of Long King—*mikko,* "chief," often rendered "mingo" in English—of the Texas Coushattas during the first three decades of the 1800s. Long King's name is also perpetuated in Long King's Creek, which Tempe Creek joins just downstream from this site.

To reach **Indian Hill** from **Long King's Village,** return to U.S. 190; take U.S. 190 west about 4 miles to the FM 2457 intersection; take FM

2457 west about 4.6 miles, to the water's edge at Lake Livingston; from this spot, **Indian Hill** is the narrow peninsula extending into the lake in a northwest direction.

The narrow peninsula extending into Lake Livingston was once a hill overlooking the junction of Penwau Slough and the Trinity River. This **Indian Hill** is thought to have been the location of the village established by the Pakana Muskogees in 1834. The group of perhaps 150 Creek Indians had come here from Alabama via Lousiana, following the same pattern as the Alabamas and Coushattas. Later, when Frenchman John Burgess married a woman of the tribe, the Muskogees were invited to live on his survey around present Onalaska. Through the later 1800s, the Polk County Muskogee population dwindled, and in 1899, all but a few of the remaining Pakanas moved to Oklahoma to live in the Creek Nation.

Poole's Creek. Photo by Wayne J. Pate

Brazos River near Ranchería Grande. Photo by Wayne J. Pate

To reach **Kickapoo Trace** from **Indian Hill,** return to U.S. 190; take U.S. 190 west about 8.1 miles, toward Onalaska over the long bridge spanning an arm of Lake Livingston, to the road running north (right) from the highway about 0.6 miles past the west end of the bridge; take this road to follow the old **Kickapoo Trace.**

Although the Kickapoo Indians are best known in Texas today as dual occupants of Coahuila, Mexico, and the Eagle Pass, Texas, area (see chapter 3), they were also migrants to East Texas during the early 1800s, where they associated with the Cherokees, Alabamas, and Coushattas. The **Kickapoo Trace** ran ninety miles south from Kickapoo settlements in Anderson County to the Coushatta villages and trail system around the Trinity River. Joining Lake Livingston near the route of the trace, Kickapoo Creek apparently takes its name from the trail and not from any known Kickapoo settlement in this area, which was dominated by the Coushattas during the period. The Pakana Muskogees who lived near Kickapoo Creek were sometimes mistakenly referred to as Kickapoos.

To reach **Poole's Creek** from **Kickapoo Trace,** return south to U.S. 190; take U.S. 190 west about 33 miles to the IH 45 intersection at Huntsville; take IH 45 north about 25.4 miles to the SH 21 intersection at Madisonville; take SH 21 east about 1.3 miles, to the crossing of **Poole's Creek.**

Comanche raiders killed a settler named Poole near this stream, which became known as **Poole's Creek.** Their attack came while surveyors were in the area; this fact and proximity to the spring-fed perennial stream suggest that they saw the presence of non-Indians at the site as a territorial claim that should be defended against. It is telling how often Indian attacks took place at notable landmarks.

To reach **Ranchería Grande (Little River–Brazos River junction)** from **Poole's Creek,** return to IH 45; take IH 45 north about 10 miles to the Old Stage Road intersection; take Old Stage Road west about 26.9 miles to the FM 46 intersection; take FM 46 west about 1.9 miles to the FM 391 intersection at Wheelock; take FM 391 west about 13.5 miles to the SH 6 intersection at Hearne; take SH 6 north about 1.3 miles to the intersection of FM 485 on the west (left) side of the road; take FM 465 west about 2.6 miles to the crossing of the Brazos River; this crossing is just north of the **Little River–Brazos River junction.**

Near the junction of the Little and Brazos Rivers in June 1716, the Spanish colonial Ramón Expedition out of Mexico visited the huge Indian encampment known as **Ranchería Grande.** As the Apaches moved in from the north and the Spaniards from the south, **Ranchería Grande** became mainly a camp for refugee Indians from the many groups who were experiencing disruptions of their native survival patterns. A local Tonkawa group called Cantona was joined here by Indians from several Coahuiltecan bands, including the Ervipiame, Mescal, Mesquite, Pamaya, Payaya, Sijame, Ticmamar, and Xarame, as well as others. The majority of the refugees came from southern Texas, below the Balcones Escarpment, and also from the Mexican state of Coahuila, where Apache and Spanish pressure bore from each direction. (Friars traveling with the Ramón Expedition recognized many Indians at Ranchería Grande who formerly lived at the missions along the Rio Grande.) Expedition notes indicate that the environment here—then characterized by a wooded creek valley, surrounding tall grass of the blackland prairie, and bison herds—was rich enough to support some two thousand Indians, along with their horses and dogs, living away to the east from the main thrust of alien intrusion.

3

SOUTH TEXAS

Away from bustling Corpus Christi and the craziness of Padre Island during spring break, much of South Texas is a forlorn and mysterious landscape where secrets whisper in the breezes. Among those secrets are traces of the Texas Indian past, a past that always seems less accessible here than in other regions of the state.

The sojourns of Cabeza de Vaca during 1528 to 1536 and of René Robert Cavelier, Sieur de La Salle, in the 1680s among South Texas Indians provide some of the earliest records of Native life in Texas, while very recent advances in the archaeology and history of the area are leading to a much more refined understanding. But for South Texas there was no concerted struggle between horse Indians and Anglo pioneers, so there is no body of literature comparable to the U.S. Army explorers' journals and fort records that tell us so much about Indian trails and camps in the West Texas plains and mountains.

The Euro-American conquest of South Texas was subtle by comparison, though no less harsh. It was a largely civilian campaign of displacement, discrimination, and forced assimilation. It began much earlier than the famous Indian Wars, and it was also more final—final in the sense that federally recognized groups of Coahuiltecan and Karankawa Indians no longer exist and final in the sense that individuals who can demonstrate descent from these tribes are very rare anymore.

The Karankawas were inhabitants of the coastal areas, whereas the Coahuiltecans generally lived in the interior plains and brush. Despite some differing food sources and organizing strategies, these peoples were much alike, hunter–gatherers who were very skillful in exploiting their environments. Deer and bison were important to both groups, and both enjoyed harvests of nuts and prickly pear fruit. The coast provided shellfish, fish, and alligators to the Karankawas, who used dugout canoes and who also showed a keen understanding of seasonal changes when traveling to or from the shoreline to hunt and harvest.

Five large subgroups of Karankawan people corresponded to the large areas between the major rivers up and down the coast, and these units broke into lower-order groupings as needed. Away from the coast, food was scarcer, and the Coahuiltecans were masters at maximizing very limited resources. They often depended on rabbits and even smaller game. They tended to forage in smaller groups, forming hundreds of small Coahuiltecan bands, with many names recorded by the Spanish and many more undoubtedly forgotten.

Tonkawas also ventured into South Texas, as did relative late-comers the Apaches and Comanches. Some Tonkawas apparently intermarried with Karankawas during the disruptions of the early 1800s. For the plains horse nomads, South Texas was a place for the occasional raid or a stopover on the way to Mexico. The most famous of their adventures was the August 1840 Comanche raid on the port of Linnville, present-day Calhoun County (described on p. 79).

The lifeways of the Coahuiltecans were upset early in the historic period by the Apaches, Comanches, and Spanish. Many Coahuil-tecans sought protection from the horse Indians within the walls of Spanish missions. A lot of these people became at least nomi-nal converts to Catholicism and thus assimilated to a generalized Hispanic society that was developing at the time. During the mid- to late 1700s, other Coahuiltecans occupied what were essentially refugee camps in the narrow no-man's land between the Apache and Spanish domains.

The Karankawas were more successful at avoiding Spanish pressures. When Karankawas did come in to the missions, it was

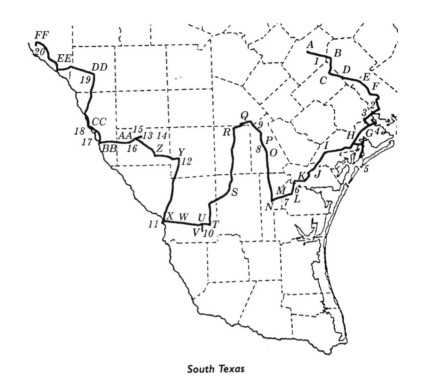

South Texas

Sites

1. Big Hill
2. Red Bluff
3. Placedo Creek
4. Linnville
5. Blackjack Peninsula
6. Santa Margarita Crossing
7. Agua Dulce Creek
8. Comanche Hills
9. Lipan Hills
10. Los Ojuelos
11. Indian Crossing at Fort McIntosh
12. Los Raices Creek
13. Comanche Crossing
14. Indian Mound
15. Soldier Slough
16. Carrizo Springs
17. Kickapoo Village
18. International Bridge, Eagle Pass
19. Las Moras Springs
20. Seminole Canyon

Cities and Towns

A. Gonzalez
B. Shiner
C. Yoakum
D. Hope
E. Morales
F. Edna
G. Port Lavaca
H. Tivoli
I. Refugio
J. Sinton
K. Odem
L. Banquete
M. Agua Dulce
N. Alice
O. George West
P. Three Rivers
Q. Campbellton
R. Cross
S. Freer
T. Bruni
U. Oilton
V. Mirando City
W. Aguilares
X. Laredo
Y. Artesia Wells
Z. Catarina
AA. Carrizo Springs
BB. El Indio
CC. Eagle Pass
DD. Brackettville
EE. Del Rio
FF. Comstock

a temporary move—they simply learned to include these resource-rich locales among other places where food could be found in their seasonal rounds. Even so, diseases introduced by Europeans appear to have become rampant among the Karankawas during the 1700s, and their numbers began to decline. As Anglos began settling land grants on the coastal prairie in the 1820s, Karankawa extinction was a foregone conclusion. In the press of the day the Karankawas were portrayed as giant tattooed cannibals who would forever remain treacherous. Soon, even small remnant bands were being hounded out of existence.

In South Texas, the breeze murmurs with sadness. Historically minded travelers can reimagine much of the drama by viewing a number of documented sites. Along the way, they are bound to feel admiration for the Native people who were able to survive and then prosper for many generations in this difficult environment.

LAY OF THE LAND

The South Texas region is part of the vast Gulf Coastal Plain of the southern United States. Within this region, the delta of the Rio Grande is sometimes treated separately as the "Rio Grande Embayment," and the interior prairie is known historically as the "Wild Horse Desert." All of these areas are coastal lowlands, ascending from the Gulf of Mexico to no more than 950 feet above sea level at the western edges along the Balcones Escarpment. The Gulf Coastal Plain continues to the north and east in Texas, but this section is treated separately as East Texas because of its heavy forests and different Indian populations.

The region is based on rock and soil deposits of a relatively young geological age, from the Tertiary and Pleistocene eras—less than about eighty million years ago—with the newest material found closest to the ocean. On the surface, two landscapes mainly make up the South Texas region: the interior brush country and a coastal zone that includes prairie, river woodlands, marshes, and dunes. This environmental split correlates with the two somewhat different adaptive regimes of the Coahuiltecans and Karankawas.

Much of the brush country was open grassland until the 1870s or after. Domesticated livestock, and for a time feral longhorns and mustangs, churned up the dense turf enough to allow the seeds of brush plants to sprout and spread. Prior to ranching days, fires started by lightning or Indians also kept the scrub down, but fire control has contributed to the expansion of the brush. Huisache, huajilla, mesquite, retama, and catclaw are some of the aggressive thorny shrubs that have come to dominate the countryside. Oaks, yucca, cactus, and grasses such as bunch grass and grama are found amid the chaparral.

The diverse coastal zone includes an interior of gently swelling prairies and dunes, much of which is now also overgrown with brush. Marsh grass and salt grass predominate. Here and there, clusters of live oak called *motts* (a southwestern term, from the Spanish *mata,* "a cover") stand out on the horizon. Buffalo ranged even this close to the shore; the first one observed by a non-Indian in Texas was seen by Cabeza de Vaca somewhere near Corpus Christi. Toward the shoreline, the country becomes difficult for travelers without a boat. Along the edges of the mainland are estuaries, lagoons, and marshes; beyond these, shallow bays and low barrier islands separate the bays from the open gulf.

Imagine the present shore landscape with no water towers or multistory hotels, and it is easy to see how the occasional high dune or mott would take on special importance as a navigation marker. It might be reasonable to suggest that the Indians living here were more attuned to the horizontal lay of the land than other people were. Perhaps they were especially good at recognizing the pattern of inlets and points along the coast; or, like the Polynesian navigators, they could sense position and direction by observing currents and the sounds that breaking waves made on the beach. We will never be able to retrieve their mind-set, but it seems clear that they did have an intimate knowledge of this potentially confusing landscape and, for a long time, enjoyed refuge from Euro-Americans because of it.

In general, South Texas is a sunny, semiarid region, but the weather is variable. The mean annual temperature is seventy degrees or more, with the weather being warm to hot, except for the occasional cold front. Snow and hard freezes are rare. Annual rainfall varies from forty inches around the northeast limit of the region at Matagorda Bay, to less than twenty inches along the Rio Grande west of Laredo. Apart from humidity along the coast, the air is dry, and steady winds speed the evaporation rate.

Tropical storms do bring heavy doses of rain in late summer and early fall. About once every ten years, a major hurricane lands along the South Texas coast. These are among the most powerful storm systems on earth, and they can be devastating. Hurricanes can radically reshape the barrier islands, cutting new passes from the bays to the open ocean. Ordinary inland rainfall also has an effect on the region, though it is indirect and less dramatic. The variable flow of fresh water from the interior into the bays affects the clarity and salinity of the bay water, which in turn influences the presence of fish and mollusks.

Across the coastal plain, the effect of variable rainfall is now compounded by farming and ranching practices: the naturalist Roy Bedichek pointed out that the creeks of South Texas look very different than they once did—the silt that washes in because of plowing and overgrazing has turned clear, powerful streams into mud-choked sloughs. The rapidly advancing polar cold fronts called "blue northers" hit South Texas several times each winter. Once in a while, a norther will cause a sudden temperature plunge in the bay waters that kills huge numbers of fish. Such fish kills would have been major harvest opportunities for Native people.

Thus, three features of the South Texas climate will dominate the impressions of anyone who spends much time there: the oppressive heat, the steady wind, and the capricious nature of the weather. The impact of the legendary South Texas heat becomes apparent when one asks long-term residents of the region what is their favorite month. They typically get a wistful look in their eyes and respond quietly but passionately, "February!" In 1989, a group of Austinites attended a weeklong meeting in Kingsville in late July. When they returned to work the following Monday, their colleagues who had not made the trip were amused to hear the travelers comment on how cool and pleasant the sweltering mornings in Austin now felt to them after a week in South Texas.

Perhaps the most telling comment about the South Texas wind comes from a veteran elementary school teacher in the Coastal Bend area. He says he can always identify children who are new to the area by their artwork: Newcomer students draw scenes of chimneys and refinery smokestacks with smoke or steam curling lazily up into the heavens, while children who are natives invariably depict smoke or steam traveling flat, parallel to the horizon. As for the capriciousness of the weather, a radio deejay in the Corpus Christi area summed up this subject well: "South Texas is the only place I know where a thunderstorm will come up to the city limits, split in two, go around town, and meet up again on the other side."

With all its drawbacks, the South Texas region has always held some appeal to human groups. It was obviously a place of some security for Indian people, even with all the hardships and especially before the coming of Euro-Americans. Pioneers from Mexico saw a land of opportunity and hence established the basis for modern civilization in the region. The population and regional culture are still heavily Hispanic, overwhelmingly so along the Rio Grande. The Rio Grande Valley, known simply as "the Valley," presents a fascinating modern landscape of intense, continuous urban development. Irrigation and the railroad spurred development here after 1900, and immigration from Latin America has fed growth in recent decades. Irrigation was also key to the establishment of the so-called Winter Garden area in the counties north of Laredo, a center for year-round vegetable production.

Famous for its cotton, vegetable, and citrus farms, and for its cattle concerns such as the enormous King Ranch, South Texas now looks also to *maquiladoras* and transportation centers for economic security. Meanwhile, a climate deemed hot and dry by those close to the land appears simply "mild" to some modern folks. Nowadays, the Rio Grande Valley is the winter destination for thousands of "snowbirds," long-term vacationers from the upper Midwest; and in March, the beaches are overrun with college students on spring break. Travelers interested in Texas's Indian heritage will find certain evidence even in these busy settings, but the many square miles of remote brush are more evocative of the historic past.

People who have spent time in South Texas either love it or hate it, and residents of the region take a perverse pride in the intensity and range of reactions that their homeland provokes in others. As modern natives sometimes say, "It's not the end of the world, but you *can* see it from here!"

EXPLORING SOUTH TEXAS

The South Texas route begins between Gonzalez and Shiner, two towns that lie on U.S. 90A. **Big Hill** is the prominent ridge that is crested by U.S. 90A, 13 miles east of Gonzalez and 5.5 miles west of Shiner.

Much of what we know about Indian navigation in the South Texas area comes from pioneer accounts dating to the years before the Civil War, when raids and retaliations by whites and Indians were part of everyday life. During this era, settlers noted the Indian habit of scouting the coastal plain from the pronounced ridge along the west edge of the lowlands before embarking on raids on settlements below. This mild escarpment, called **Big Hill** or McClure's Hill, extends for many miles, running northeast to southwest, with several high spots along the way. John Henry Brown, a chronicler of Indian–pioneer conflict, wrote that circa 1840 "Indian raiders, bound below, almost invariably crossed the Columbus and Gonzales road at the most conspicuous elevation of this ridge."

To reach **Red Bluff** from **Big Hill,** take U.S. 90A east about 5.5 miles to the SH 95 intersection at Shiner; take SH 95 south about 8 miles to the ALT SH 77 intersection; take ALT SH 77 about 1.8 miles to the SH 111 intersection at Yoakum; take SH 111 east through Yoakum; follow Grand Street east for 9 blocks, then Gonzales Street south for 2 blocks, then go east again on SH 111; take SH 111 about 48.5 miles through Hope, Morales, and Edna, and across Lake Texana, to the FM 1593 intersection; take FM 1593 south about 9 miles to the FM 616 intersection at Lolita; take FM 616 2.2 miles to the bridge over the Navidad and Lavaca River confluence, marked "Lavaca River"; look north from the bridge along the Navidad River (the stream to the east or right) to see **Red Bluff,** a subtle rise appearing as a line of trees on the far horizon on the east side of the river about 1.5 miles away; closer approaches off of CR 429 running north from Lolita put the driver on the back slope of the bluff so that the feature is no more apparent than from the Lavaca River bridge.

Archaeological evidence about the Karankawas shows that they favored uplands over river plains when setting up their hunting camps. Such locations would have given them firmer ground to camp on, protection from flash floods and ambush, and perhaps a better view of the countryside for spotting game. According to local tradition, before European settlers came to the area in the 1830s, the top of **Red Bluff** was used as a camping place by Karankawa Indians. The forty-foot red clay bluff rises along the east bank of the Navidad River just downstream from where the Palmetto Bend Dam forms Lake Texana. An Anglo community was established at the bluff, but it faded, leaving only a cemetery. Carancahua Creek—running south to the bay of the same name, only about ten miles east of Red Bluff—also attests to the presence of the coast-dwelling Karankawa people in this area.

To reach **Placedo Creek** from **Red Bluff,** continue on FM 616 from the Lavaca River bridge about 14 miles, through Vanderbilt and La Salle and over Garcitas Creek to the bridge at **Placedo Creek.**

Upstream from this crossing on **Placedo Creek** is where the Comanches who raided Linnville (see next entry) camped on August 7, 1840, the night before their attack. The creek and nearby community bear the misspelled name of Plácido Benavides, who was actually a settler and rancher who came to the area after 1828.

To reach the site of **Linnville** from **Placedo Creek,** continue on FM 616 about 4.5 to the U.S. 87 intersection beyond the town of Placedo; take U.S. 87 south about 12.8 miles through Kamey to the SH 35 intersection at Port Lavaca; take SH 35 north about 1.5 miles to the FM 1090 intersection; take FM 1090 west (northwest, left) about 2.6 miles to the Maxwell Ditch Road intersection (the road sign reads only "Maxwell"); take Maxwell Ditch Road north (northeast) about 1 mile to the Bay

Placedo Creek. Photo by Daniel J. Gelo

Meadow Road intersection on the east (southeast, right) side of the road; take Bay Meadow Road southeast and northeast about 1 mile to the waterfront; the shoreline southeast of the road is the former site of the town of **Linnville.**

Linnville was a thriving shipping center on Lavaca Bay when it was destroyed on August 8, 1840, by Comanche raiders who were bent on revenge after a parlay gone sour in San Antonio, the infamous Council House Fight. With the possible urging of Mexican agents, five hundred Penateka Comanche warriors with their families in tow swept down the Guadalupe River Valley all the way from the Hill Country to the coast. They attacked Victoria and outlying farms before surrounding the port of Linnville. Most of the two hundred residents fled onto the bay in boats, beyond the reach of Comanche arrows, and they watched as the Indians pillaged and burned their houses, shops, and warehouses all day long. At Plum Creek (near present-day Lockhart, Caldwell County), volunteers overtook the Comanches on their way home and gave them a trouncing that put an end to any more big coastal raids. But the attack demonstrated the long reach and might of the Comanche Nation during the era. Only one Linnville building was left standing, and the town was never rebuilt. Part of the present town site is now under water.

To reach **Blackjack Peninsula** from the site of **Linnville,** return to SH 35 at Port Lavaca via FM 1090; take SH 35 south (southwest) about 21 miles through Tivoli to the second SH 239 intersection on the east (left) side of the road; take SH 239 south (southeast) about 4.7 miles to the SH 774 intersection in Austwell; take SH 774 south about 0.6 miles to the FM 2040 intersection; take FM 2040 east (south) about 6.4 miles to the entrance of **Aransas National Wildlife Refuge** and beyond, which is where you can find **Blackjack Peninsula.**

The **Blackjack Peninsula** is characteristic of the coastal bay environment that was attractive to many tribes, and the **Aransas National Wildlife Refuge** preserves some sense of what the landscape looked like before Indians were driven from the area in the early 1800s. The peninsula was a campsite at various times for Tonkawas, Lipan Apaches, and Comanches, who (surprisingly) may have ventured all the way here from their more northwesterly Texas homelands. This environment, though, was most typical for the coast-dwelling Karankawas. Harboring a wide variety of game

Santa Margarita Crossing. Photo by Daniel J. Gelo

animals and birds, the peninsula combines ponds, coastal and fresh-water marshes, and coastal prairie and oak motts.

To reach **Santa Margarita Crossing** from **Blackjack Peninsula**, return north on FM 2040 to the SH 35 intersection; take SH 35 south about 7.5 miles to the FM 774 intersection; take FM 774 west about 21 miles to the SH 77 intersection at Refugio; take SH 77 south about 31 miles through Woodsboro and Sinton to the SH 234 intersection at Odem; take SH 234 north (west) about 6 miles, underneath IH 37 to Edroy, where SH 234 turns north a short distance to join IH 37; continue northwest straight through Edroy (along the railroad tracks the road becomes CR 50 and alternates between paved and unpaved) about 7.6 miles to the CR 1168 intersection on the west (left) side of the road; take CR 1168 west about 0.8 miles to the FM 666 intersection; take FM 666 south about 6.5 miles, beyond San Patricio, to the Nueces River crossing.

The FM 666 bridge over the Nueces River at San Patricio replaces an ancient ford called Paso Santa Margarita, or **Santa**

Margarita Crossing. This site was a favored place for game animals and for Indians seeking their way across. Later it became a point on the Old San Antonio Road that linked Mexico with East Texas and Louisiana. Spanish and Mexican commerce gave way as Anglo cotton merchants and cowboys adopted the trail. A ferry was operated here from the 1860s to 1898, when a bridge was built. Upstream from this point were two or three other shallow crossings where the riverbed was rocky and used at low-water times. Local tradition says that the rocks were the flint used by Indians to make arrowheads. The farthest of these crossings, three miles upstream, was called De Leon Crossing by the Spaniards, and the west bank at this ford was a known campsite of the Lipan Apaches. Spanish and Mexican forts stood at this site in the 1700s and 1800s.

To reach **Agua Dulce Creek** from **Santa Margarita Crossing,** continue south from the Nueces River bridge on FM 666 about 9 miles to the SH 44 intersection at Banquete; take SH 44 west about 1.4 miles; at this point, the road crosses **Agua Dulce Creek.**

According to Texas Ranger Rip Ford, who had many years' experience as an Indian fighter throughout Texas, **Agua Dulce** (sweet water) was a notorious hideout for Plains Indian raiders who ventured toward the coast in the early and mid-1800s. The name itself and old accounts suggest that fresh water could once be found here in abundance, although the stream is now intermittent for most of its length. The creek lay off the main routes of travel between white settlements and would have been the perfect staging area for coastal forays by the inland Indians.

To reach **Comanche Hills** from **Agua Dulce Creek,** continue west from the Agua Dulce Creek crossing on SH 44 about 17 miles, through the town of Agua Dulce, to the U.S. 281 intersection at Alice; take U.S. 281 north about 55 miles through George West and Three Rivers to the IH 37 intersection; take IH 37 north about 2 miles, to the point where the highway crests a sizeable hill; from this point, **Comanche Hills** can be seen about 1 mile due west (left), appearing as a subtle west-facing escarpment; a safer view can be had from the rest area on the rise along the highway 1.5 miles north of this point, but the Comanche Hills are less obvious from this direction.

To reach **Lipan Hills** from **Comanche Hills,** continue north on IH 37 for about 11 to 12.5 miles; the highway crests the **Lipan Hills,** which run northeast-southwest, in this area.

The Three Rivers area where the Atascosa, Frio, and Nueces run together would have been a favorable place for Indian hunting and camping. One of the problems that the coastal plains presented to Indian people was that *chert,* the stone material for toolmaking so plentiful in the Hill Country, was hard to come by in the lowlands. The hills in the Three Rivers locality, however, are part of the subtle limestone escarpment that sweeps for many miles along the plains (see **Big Hill,** p. 76), and this limestone contains chert deposits.

IH 37 at Lipan Hills, view from the north. Photo by Daniel J. Gelo

This ready source of stone and the relatively sheltered, well-watered landscape here would have been very attractive to any Indian settlers or travelers.

Some of the better camping locations were probably submerged when Choke Canyon Reservoir was built in the 1980s. But Spanish colonial records indicate that during the late 1700s the area was the favorite camping place of the Lipan Apaches. According to the colonial reports, multiple camps were occasionally seen in the area at the same time.

Several hills in this vicinity are likely to have been used by Indian lookouts, and they can be seen via IH 37. The **Comanche Hills** rise about fifty feet above the elevation of the highway at the viewing point, though 120 feet above the Atascosa River channel that runs between the highway and the hills. A nearby creek and lake are also called "Comanche." Comanche activity at these sites has not been verified in historical records, however. The **Lipan Hills** take their name from Apache activity in the area.

To reach **Los Ojuelos** from **Lipan Hills,** continue north on IH 37 about 0.8 miles to the SH 1099 intersection; take SH 1099 west about 0.5 miles to the ALT 281 intersection; take ALT 281 north about 2 miles, through Campbellton, to the FM 140 intersection on the west (left) side of the road; take FM 140 west about 14.5 miles, through Christine, to the SH 16 intersection; take SH 16 south about 64 miles to the U.S. 59 intersection at Freer; take U.S. 59 west (southwest) about 16 miles to the FM 2050 intersection on the south (left) side of the road; take FM 2050 south about 25 miles to the SH 359 intersection at Bruni; take SH 359 west about 10.5 miles, through Oilton, to the FM 649 intersection; take FM 649 south about 4 miles, through Mirando City; **Los Ojuelos** lies a short distance east (left) of the road.

Los Ojuelos was once the location of a regular Indian camping place, owing to the dependability of several springs at the site—the best water for many dozens of miles in the harsh, arid scrub—and the wood and good grass that the fountains supported. Texas Ranger Rip Ford called **Los Ojuelos** "a great resort for the Indians," and in 1850, Ford's ranger company set up a station here to discourage Indian raiding in the area. The Indians that the rangers were concerned with at this time were presumably Lipan Apaches and Comanches, though Coahuiltecans and other peoples undoubtedly used the site, dating far back into prehistory.

Mexicans tried to settle the spot as early as 1810 under a Spanish land grant, but they were driven away by Indian attacks until the rangers brought sufficient security to the area. In 1857, a descendant of the original Mexican pioneers returned and built enough improvements to draw a community of some four hundred Mexican settlers. At this time, the springs were enclosed in stone. Beginning in the early 1920s, an oil boom at the nearby Mirando City fields led to further growth of the town, but the growth was only temporary. The springs were eventually pumped dry, and the town was soon abandoned.

To reach **Indian Crossing at Fort McIntosh (Laredo)** from **Los Ojuelos**, return north on FM 649 to the SH 359 intersection; take SH 359 west about 30 miles to the merge with U.S. 83 in Laredo; take U.S. 83, which becomes Guadalupe Street in town, north (and then west) about 2 miles, past the IH 35 intersection and three blocks past the U.S. 81 (Convent Avenue) intersection to the Santa Maria Avenue intersection; take Santa Maria Avenue north (right) for three blocks to the Washington Street intersection; take Washington Street west about 0.6 miles. **Fort McIntosh** can be found on the north side of the Laredo Junior College at the foot of Washington Street. **Indian Crossing** was on the Rio Grande adjacent to the fort.

Indian Crossing on the west side of Laredo was the farthest downriver of the important Rio Grande Indian fords, and it was used frequently by Lipan Apaches and Comanches in the heyday of their raiding in South Texas and Mexico. The crossing was a continuation of the pathway of Native travel corresponding to modern IH 35. Fort McIntosh was begun in 1849 following the Mexican War as a successor to a Spanish presidio. It became part of the twin line of forts that the U.S. government established to monitor the Texas frontier. The celebrated Indian fighter Rip Ford was stationed here for a time, as were U.S. Army officers Randolph B. Marcy and Phil Sheridan, both famous for their dealings elsewhere with Texas Indians.

To reach **Los Raices Creek** from **Indian Crossing at Fort McIntosh,** return to IH 35; take IH 35 north about 56 miles to the SH 133 intersection at Artesia Wells; the washes crossed on IH 35 in approaching this intersection and the one immediately north of the intersection are prongs of **Los Raices Creek.**

Another of the Indian-raid staging areas that Texas Ranger Rip Ford listed was "Raices Creek," almost certainly **Los Raices Creek** (*raices,* "the roots," or perhaps "the origins"). Again, this area would have been a stopover for Apaches and Comanches intent on attacking the settlements of South Texas and Mexico, though the water hole would have hosted other earlier groups, too. This tributary is one of several from the middle Nueces River that appears to have offered decent water and wood to Indian travelers. As the community name Artesia Wells suggests, subsurface water was once abundant around the head of Los Raices, and it is no accident that the road between San Antonio and Laredo comes right through this locality. The town was originally a railroad water stop and later a center for Winter Garden farming activity. Now only a few dozen people live here.

To reach **Comanche Crossing** and **Indian Mound** from **Los Raices Creek,** take FM 133 west about 20.5 miles to the U.S. 83 intersection at Catarina; take U.S. 83 north about 20.6 miles to the SH 85 intersection at Carrizo Springs on the east (right) side of the highway; take SH 85 east about 6.8 miles to a roadside park on the north (left) side of the highway; looking east from this point, one sees **Comanche Crossing** of the Nueces River; **Indian Mound** is the slope that SH 85 road tops east of this crossing.

The Nueces River crossing at SH 85 is the probable location of an Indian ford known to the Texas Rangers as **Comanche Crossing.** A narrow impoundment called Bermuda Lake, which actually appears more like a river than a lake, has flooded the river channel here and, along with highway and bridge construction, has altered the appearance of the crossing. But this ford would have been an excellent pathway between the Hill Country and Mexico, especially with fresh water close by at Carrizo Springs. Another advantage

Comanche Crossing of the Nueces River. Photo by Daniel J. Gelo

of this spot was the adjacent hill called **Indian Mound,** which allows a well-marked, safe approach to the ford and a survey of the countryside for many miles to the north, east, and south.

To reach **Soldier Slough** from **Comanche Crossing** and **Indian Mound,** return west on SH 85 about 2 miles; **Soldier Slough** can be seen at this point running north-south under the highway.

Further evidence of the level of Indian activity in this area is provided by the place name **Soldier Slough** (and Soldier Lake, the impoundment on the slough one mile south of the viewing point). According to local tradition, the name stems from an 1870s engagement in which two soldiers were killed by Indians. About 2.6 direct miles north-northwest of the viewing point, Espantosa Lake drains into Soldier Slough. This lake is natural and has been the focus of many legends about ghosts and lost treasure. The Spanish name *Espantosa* means "frightful" or "terrifying." Given widespread Indian beliefs that sluggish water holes and other low places are the abodes of dangerous spirits, it is very likely that these local legends are continuations of Native beliefs about the place.

> To reach **Carrizo Springs** from **Soldier Slough,** return to the U.S.
> 83 intersection; take U.S. 83 (North 1st Street) two blocks south to the
> U.S. 277 (Pena Street) intersection on the west (right) side of the road;
> take U.S. 277 north (west) about 1.1 miles to the city limits; from this
> point, the main **Carrizo Springs** were found southwest of the road at
> a distance of about 0.3 miles.

A line of springs once ran through the town **Carrizo Springs,** where Coahuiltecan Indians established their villages. The spring flow has declined dramatically in the past hundred years. Although "Carrizo," or "Karisu," is a name that was applied to historic Coahuiltecan and Apache bands, the name here is more literal, referring in Spanish to the reeds that grew around the creek that was fed by the springs.

> To reach the **Kickapoo Village** from **Carrizo Springs,** continue on
> U.S. 277 about 0.5 miles to the FM 2644 intersection on the west (left)
> side of the road; take FM 2644 west about 27 miles to the FM 1021
> intersection at El Indio; take FM 1021 about 12 miles to the Rosita
> Valley Road intersection on the west (left) side of the road; take Rosita
> Valley Road about 2 miles to the **Kickapoo Village.**

One of three Indian reservations in Texas today is the **Kickapoo Village,** southeast of Eagle Pass. This community was established in the 1980s as a home for the so-called Mexican Kickapoo Indians. (see next entry). Ancestors of this branch of the Kickapoo Indians migrated into Texas in the early 1800s from their homeland near the Great Lakes. From Texas, many continued to El Nacimiento, Coahuila, some 130 miles southwest of Eagle Pass, where in 1852 the Mexican government furnished them with land for a settlement.

For part of the year, many of the Mexican Kickapoos also reside around Eagle Pass, their traditional crossing place between Mexico and Texas, when seeking wage work. Despite their dual status as citizens of Mexico and Texas and despite their work throughout the United States as migrant laborers, the Mexican Kickapoos have

Kickapoo traditional dwellings, El Nacimiento, Coahuila. Until recently, these houses were also built at Eagle Pass, Texas. Photo by Daniel J. Gelo

tended to stay away from non-Indian schools, churches, and other institutions. They tend to speak Kickapoo or Spanish more than English, although many are fully trilingual. As a result, the Mexican Kickapoos have been able to preserve their native Algonkian language, religion, and clan system to a greater degree than probably any other American Indian group living in the United States. At Kickapoo Village, however, traditional sapling and reed dwellings have given way to brick houses over the past ten years, and a new tribally operated casino regularly brings outsiders to the community.

To reach the **International Bridge at Eagle Pass** from the **Kickapoo Village,** return to FM 1021; take FM 1021 north (west) about 6.5 to the U.S. 57 (Garrison Street) intersection at Eagle Pass; take U.S. 57 west a few blocks toward the **International Bridge** that crosses the Rio Grande; pull off onto one of the side streets north (right) of U.S. 57 near the river to avoid having to cross the bridge into Mexico.

Beneath the **International Bridge at Eagle Pass** is a broad section of Rio Grande flood plain that served as the most recent notable Indian camping place in Texas history. Between the 1940s and the 1980s, Kickapoo Indians maintained a sizeable village of Native-style dwellings at this location. The houses were built according to Kickapoo custom with lashed sapling frameworks. When the traditional building material of river reeds was not available to them, they substituted plastic sheeting, large pieces of cardboard from shipping boxes, and the like. There was no indoor plumbing.

Floodwaters periodically surged through the village, ruining the houses and leaving mud and debris. These circumstances produced what appeared to be a shantytown that drew the condemnation of other area residents. Pressure mounted for the Kickapoos to abandon the site. Fortunately, after 1977, these Indians won state and federal recognition, as well as unambiguous American citizenship. Funds were thus raised for them to buy tribal land in Texas. By 1989, the inhabitants of the International Bridge village were able to move to the present Kickapoo Village community, which is downriver on high ground.

To reach **Las Moras Springs at Fort Clark Springs** from the **International Bridge at Eagle Pass,** return east and north on U.S. 57 to U.S. 57/U.S. 277 (Main Street); take U.S. 57/U.S. 277 east one block to Ceylon Street on the left side of the road, which is U.S. 277 northbound; take U.S. 277 north about 12 miles to the SH 131 intersection on the east (right) side of the highway; take SH 131 north about 33 miles, through Spofford, to the U.S. 90 intersection at Brackettville; proceed on U.S. 90 east less than 0.4 miles to Bowie Road, the entrance to the Fort Clarke Springs private resort community on the south (left) side of highway; take Bowie Road a short distance to Swim Park Lane on the west (right) side of the road; follow Swim Park Lane about 0.6 miles to view **Las Moras Springs.**

Las Moras Springs, the ninth-largest spring system in the state, served prehistoric and historic Indians as well as Spanish colonists traveling between El Paso and San Antonio. In 1840, cavalry drove off Comanches camping at the springs. Lieutenant William Henry Chase Whiting rediscovered the springs in 1849 while exploring an east-west route for the U.S. Army Corps of Engineers. Whiting wrote in his journal that the springs were hidden in a dense grove of pecans and mulberries, and he noted as a landmark Las Moras Mountain, rising to the northeast at a distance of about 3.5 miles:

> About three miles off stands the hill, a remarkable feature of the country. It is of no great elevation, not being higher than the table formation farther to the north, but it rises solitary with its two eminences from the midst of a beautiful plain of great extent. It is a favorite lookout of the Indians, and many trails for Mexican depredation come by this point from the upper Nueces, the Llano, and the San Saba. (Bieber and Bender 1938, p. 348)

Fort Clark was established here in 1852 as the southernmost in a line of forts intended to monitor Indian traffic and guard settlers; it remained an active post until 1944. At Fort Clark were stationed many of the Black Seminole scouts recruited to guide the army campaigns against the Kickapoos, Comanches, and Kiowas in the 1870s (see **Seminole Draw,** chapter 6, p. 156). These were largely former African American slaves of Seminole Indians in Florida and their mixed-blood descendants who had been relocated in Oklahoma, Texas, and Mexico. As brave trackers and fighters familiar with English, Spanish, and multiple Indian languages, they provided effective service in the borderlands. The Black Seminoles who were attached to Fort Clark lived in Seminole Camp along Las Moras Creek south of the springs when they were not out on patrol. After the scout units were disbanded in 1912, they moved into Brackettville and maintained a community that still exists.

To reach **Seminole Canyon** from **Las Moras Springs,** return to U.S. 90; take U.S. 90 west about 71 miles, through Del Rio and Comstock, to the entrance to **Seminole Canyon State Historical Park** on the south (left) side of the road, clearly marked by highway signs on the north side of the road.

Seminole Canyon is a place to learn about the landscape that once supported stable populations of early humans. Around the Pecos and Devil's River just above their junctions with the Rio Grande a culture of Archaic hunter–gatherers flourished between six and one thousand years ago. The people of the Lower Pecos left much evidence of a lifestyle based on the hunting of rabbits and the collection of wild seeds and roots. In the caves above the riverbeds, naturally mummified human bodies and their belongings, such as sandals skillfully woven from yucca fiber, have been found preserved in the dry heat.

Equally arresting is the pictographic rock art common in these locations, showing a fantastic array of spirits and animals on the cave shelter walls—all evidence of a rich life of imagination and religion. At **Seminole Canyon State Historical Park,** visitors can take guided hikes to approach some of the key locations, such as the Fate Bell Shelter. Some of the hikes are long and strenuous, so it is best to plan ahead and budget extra time for a visit here; call (915) 292-4464 for information.

Seminole Canyon belongs as much to the Hill Country and the Mountains and Basins region as it does to South Texas; it is the end point for the South Texas tour. Travelers can return to the Gonzalez area starting point by taking U.S. 90, IH 10, and U.S. 90A east through Del Rio and San Antonio, a distance of about 258 miles.

4

THE HILL COUNTRY

No area of Texas is more renowned for its natural beauty than the Hill Country in the center of the state, and perhaps no other area enjoys such a distinct identity. Sometimes subtle and other times dramatic, the scenery features sparkling creeks, pastoral landscapes, and occasional long vistas. Summer temperatures run cooler here than they do in the adjacent plains, but winters are still relatively mild because the hilly terrain slows the worst of the northern winds. The inviting climate and an environment somewhat reminiscent of Europe and the eastern United States drew Euro-American settlers in significant numbers in the twenty years prior to the Civil War.

The common notion of a distinct Hill Country region derives in part from the history of the settlement, involving Anglo pioneers from the easterly mountain regions of Appalachia and the Ozarks. The Spanish had penetrated the area before these Anglo settlers, but never in large enough numbers to overcome Indian resistance. Another distinctive aspect of the Hill Country settlement is the concentration of Germans. Sold on the area by promoters who exaggerated its better qualities, German immigrants established farms and towns in a corridor running northwest from San Antonio and New Braunfels to Mason, roughly along the major Indian route called the Pinta Trail.

The beauty and natural advantages that were so appealing to Euro-American settlers were also attractive to Native peoples, and diverse Indian groups occupied the region. Popular history portrays the Hill Country as Comanche territory because the Comanches were the most powerful people encountered here during the days of intensive Euro-American settlement. After moving into Texas from the northwest in the 1740s, Comanches discovered the sheltered, well-watered winter pastures of the area canyons, and they began camping in them to nurture their horse herds in seclusion.

The southernmost Comanche band, the Penateka (Honey Eaters or Wasps), headquartered in the Hill Country during the first half of the nineteenth century, though other bands came through the area as well. For many Comanches, the hills were a safe haven from which to launch raiding and trading expeditions, such as those conducted each spring to Mexico. And in this central location, the Penatekas became most directly involved in the diplomacy between Indians and Euro-Americans, which developed as the line of settlement advanced. Their leaders were signatories in an 1847 treaty with German settlers that is said never to have been broken; descendants of the signers on both sides met in Fredericksburg in 1998 to celebrate the pact.

The Penateka saga is only one late aspect of Indian history in the Hill Country, however. The Comanches wrested control of central Texas from the Lipan Apaches who migrated there from the northwest ahead of them. The Lipans were vulnerable to Comanche attack because they were in the habit of returning every spring and fall to corn gardens that they maintained in the Hill Country canyons; yet, they had been successful occupants of the area for many generations. Pioneering the classic Plains Indian lifestyle of horsemanship and buffalo hunting, they persisted in the fringes of the Hill Country after the Comanche intrusion and well into the nineteenth century. It is quite likely that cultural practices considered typical of the Comanches, such as smoke signaling and use of the lance in mounted combat, were inspired by Apache example.

Apaches and Comanches both in turn oppressed the Tonkawas, a group of remnant societies that had coalesced in central Texas. The Tonkawas were long thought to have been ancient inhabitants of the area with obscure origins; in fact, newer archaeological evidence suggests that at least some components of the group might have migrated from the north as late as the 1600s. Like the Lipans, the Tonkawas pursued an early version of the plains buffalo-hunting economy, but in the records of the Spanish and Anglos, they appear as a downtrodden, marginalized people. They tried siding with the Comanches and Apaches alternately, but never gained sufficient protection in these alliances. The Comanches found the Tonkawa practice of cannibalizing fallen enemies abhorrent and derided them as *numuteka, "people eaters."*

After the mid-1800s, Tonkawas scouted for the U.S. Army on patrols against their Indian foes. Shawnee and Delaware Indians, late migrants from the east, also worked as scouts in the Hill Country, the latter at Fort Martin Scott in Fredericksburg.

Members of another tribe from the eastern woodlands, the Kickapoos of the Great Lakes area, arrived in numbers during the 1830s, some of them camping and hunting in the central hills. Coahuiltecan-speaking peoples of South Texas are also associated with the Hill Country because some bands depended on the water sources issuing from the Balcones Escarpment around present San Antonio. Similarly, the springs emerging from the Edwards Acquifer at Salado hosted the Tawakonis, a branch of the Wichita Indians from the north and east.

Visitors to the Hill Country enjoy a rich Indian legacy at every turn. Many of the modern roads here lie along a trail system that was long in place when the Comanches laid claim to it in the 1700s.

THE LAY OF THE LAND

As defined here, the Hill Country includes the Central Texas hills as well as the Edwards Plateau to the west and the Llano Basin adjacent on the northeast (the latter is a geological area of Central Texas, not to be confused with the Llano Estacado). The overall region is often called simply the Edwards Plateau, or the Hill Country, and is regarded by geographers as the southernmost extension of the High Plains physiographic province. The Hill Country gives way to the Staked Plains and Rolling Plains to the north, and to the East Texas prairies and woodlands to the northeast. West of the Edwards lies the Mountains and Basins region. On the southeast and south, the Hill Country is bounded from the lowlands by the modest rise of the Balcones Escarpment. A few of the places included in this chapter are actually off the escarpment, but these are campsites with spring water that flows from the Hill Country aquifers.

The hills proper are a kind of geological illusion in that they are really remnants of the top of a heavily dissected series of limestone plateaus. For this reason, peaks in the same extensive subarea are normally about the same height. (To the west, less erosion has occurred, and thus the Edwards Plateau remains more intact.) Overall elevations are often under a thousand feet above sea level, though it increases as one moves west. Small canyons among the hills offered shelter from wind and green grass year-round for early inhabitants. Moreover, the limestone bedrock that lies at most a few inches below the topsoil is chock full of Edwards chert, one of the very finest materials for stone toolmaking.

Several of the state's best-known streams rise here, including the Pedernales, San Saba, Devil's River, and the three branches of the Concho. Abundant, pure water lies deep underground in the Edwards and Edwards-Trinity aquifers. During rainy years, underground water finds its way to the surface in springs everywhere, particularly along and just beyond the southeast face of the escarpment.

In Indian days, the Hill Country landscape was one of open, short-grass prairie alternating with open oak forest. The setting resembled a park, as shown in the paintings of Fredericksburg residents Hermann Lungkwitz (1813–1891) and Richard Petri (1824–1857). Juniper brakes were also found on the eastern margins. The juniper and mesquite cover is seen today across wide areas; it gained its dominance once ranching and farming disturbed the native vegetation.

Buffalo were common enough here that the Comanches regarded the area as essential hunting territory. White-tailed deer, bear, and smaller animals like javelina and wild turkey once abounded here as well. The wild turkey population has been restored. Deer remain more abundant here than anywhere else in the nation, and deer hunting, as well as hunting of stocked exotic game such as African wild sheep and antelope from India, is an important part of the regional economy. For thousands of Texans, the deer (hunting) lease in the Hill Country is a family tradition. The Edwards Plateau is now also home to about two million domestic sheep, yielding seventeen million pounds of wool annually, and those seasonal visitors who are not hunters may have in mind the restful scenery around the sheep ranching towns.

The modern Hill Country is perhaps the Texas region least likely to correspond to a stereotype of Indian territory. The hilly green terrain and extensive agricultural development contribute to this effect, as do place-names that seem to underscore the influence of European cultures: San Marcos, New Braunfels, Fredericksburg. This effect does fade as the traveler moves northwest from the more densely populated and hillier southeastern section of the region.

In the westerly cedar-punctuated expanses, the region looks a little more like Indian country is supposed to look, at least when sheep are not present. The country flattens as hills become extended mesas, and canyons are replaced by broad draws, changing almost imperceptibly into the true plains. This broader terrain lent itself better to the Indian styles of horse travel, hunting, and raiding. Out here were some of the earlier (pre–Civil War) forts established by the U.S. Army to patrol for Comanche raiders—Mason, Concho, McKavett. Still, and despite its importance to Native populations, the region today is not purely evocative of the great buffalo hunts or cavalry campaigns. One can better imagine this as the place of cultural give-and-take, where Indian people faced early pressure to become "civilized" and where some Indian leaders brokered for coexistence while others led raids against missions, farmsteads, and wagoneers.

In recent years, real estate prices throughout the southern and eastern sections of the Hill Country have soared, and several small towns in the area have boomed. This is the part of Texas that urban Texans and newcomers to the state think of most often when they dream of "moving to the country." As a longtime resident of the area says, "When you see the office of a national stock brokerage firm in downtown Marble Falls, you know for a fact that the Hill Country has been discovered!" The same force of attraction that drew earlier residents is still at work, and it remains to be seen whether the natural and cultural resources, and sheer beauty, of the area can be preserved in the face of this modern colonization.

EXPLORING THE HILL COUNTRY

This tour begins west-southwest of Brady in the town of Menard, which lies at the intersection of U.S. 83 and U.S. 190. To view the site of **Mission Santa Cruz de San Saba,** take FM 2092 east from U.S. 83 about 2 miles. The mission site lies north of the highway, toward the river. To view the remains of **Real Presidio de San Saba,** visit the county park on the south side of U.S. 190 about 1 mile west of U.S. 83.

Mission Santa Cruz de San Saba was established by Spanish Franciscan missionaries for Lipan Apaches in 1757. At dawn on March 16, 1758, two thousand *Norteño* warriors (allied tribes from the north), newly armed with French guns, surrounded the mission, gained entry under some pretext, and sacked and burned it, killing many of the occupants. Although the raid has often been blamed on Comanches, the majority of attackers were Caddos, Wichitas, and Tonkawas. Nevertheless, the attack resounded in the Spanish colonial world, which had for some time feared a Comanche invasion of the Texas missions.

A fort, **Real Presidio de San Saba,** had also been built to protect the missionaries, though three miles west and on the opposite side of the river. Soldiers from the fort were ineffective in protecting the

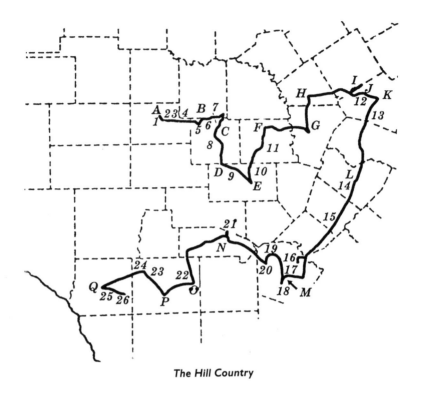

The Hill Country

Sites

1. Mission Santa Cruz de San Saba
2. Real Presidio de San Saba
3. Pegleg Crossing
4. McDougal Draw
5. Double Knobs
6. Katemcy Rocks
7. Spy's Rock
8. Todd Mountain
9. Indian Point
10. Cross Mountain
11. Enchanted Rock
12. Comanche Gap, Cedar Gap
13. Salado Springs
14. Barton Springs
15. San Marcos Springs
16. Comanche Lookout
17. San Pedro Springs
18. Chihuahua Trail
19. Paso de Los Apaches
20. Helotes
21. Bandera Pass
22. Uvalde Canyon
23. Chalk Bluff
24. West Nueces Canyon
25. Las Moras Springs
26. Anacacho Mts.

Cities and Towns

A. Menard
B. Katemcy
C. Mason
D. Doss
E. Fredericksburg
F. Llano
G. Burnet
H. Lampasas
I. Killeen
J. Nolanville
K. Belton
L. Austin
M. San Antonio
N. Bandera
O. Sabinal
P. Uvalde
Q. Brackettville

mission during the great attack, but afterward the presidio became the refuge and headquarters for those Spaniards and acolytes who stayed. The fort remained isolated by Indian depredations in the years that followed, however, and was ultimately abandoned by 1770.

Some sixty years later, the mission vicinity was still a focal point for Indian activity, as the terminus of the **Pinta Trail** running to San Antonio. During an 1828 hunt, Comanches riding with Swiss explorer and botanist Jean Louis Berlandier parted company with him and headed toward San Saba, referring in their language to the deserted Spanish presidio as "old house." Berlandier watched their progress in that direction by the smoke signals that rose along the Pinta Trail.

To reach **Pegleg Crossing** and **McDougal Draw** from **Real Presidio de San Saba,** take U.S. 190 east about 1 mile to the intersection with U.S. 83; take U.S. 83 south about 3 miles to the U.S. 83/SH 29 intersection; take SH 29 south and east about 10 miles, to a roadside park on the north side of the road; about 0.7 miles north-northeast of the park on the San Saba River is **Pegleg Crossing,** and **McDougal Draw** runs between the hills from the park to the river crossing.

This section of SH 29 is built on the **Pinta Trail** (the full route of this trail is reconstructed on p. 113). **McDougal Draw** overlooking the key ford at **Pegleg Crossing** was a common Indian campsite and the location of a battle between the Spanish and Apaches in 1732.

To reach **Double Knobs** from **Pegleg Crossing** and **McDougal Draw,** take SH 29 east approximately 16 miles; the roadway passes between **Double Knobs.**

Such double landmarks as the **Double Knobs** are rare, but they show up persistently as Indian trail markers. Note how the Pinta Trail (present SH 29) passed directly between these hills.

To reach **Katemcy Rocks** from the **Double Knobs,** return west on SH 29 2.6 miles to the intersection with FM 1222 on the north side

Katemcy Rocks with old Comanche pasture in foreground. Photo by Daniel J. Gelo

of the road; take FM 1222 north and east to its intersection with U.S. 87 **(Camp Air)**; **Katemcy Rocks** are the low, even hills southeast of this point, best viewed from U.S. 87 0.5 miles north of the Camp Air intersection.

A closer look at **Katemcy Rocks** can be had by taking FM 1222 east from the Camp Air intersection about 2.3 miles, to the community of Katemcy; this road skirts the northern face of the rocks; the canyon of **Devil's Spring** runs southeast from the roadway opposite the Katemcy community.

Katemcy Rocks is a broad granite formation running from the southwest to northeast. According to local folk history, the small gorges in this area were the winter camping places in the 1840s for the six hundred or so Penateka Comanches composing the band under Ketumsee (Ketemoczy, Katemcy). In particular, **Devil's Spring** (Devils Springs) is remembered as an Indian campsite. The flats around **Camp Air** were used for grazing by the Comanches, who periodically burned the area to promote the growth of prairie grass; in the 1850s, soldiers from Fort Mason cut hay here. In the summer, Ketumsee's group would move downstream (north) along Katemcy Creek from this location to camp along the San Saba River. Ketumsee's band was thought to cooperate at times in large buffalo hunts with the people under Santa Anna, who camped further to the east (see chapter 5).

Ketumsee played an important role in diplomacy with the advancing Anglo-Americans, and he also participated in the negotiation of the famous German–Comanche Treaty of 1847. He eventually functioned as the principal leader of all the southern Comanche bands and led them as they relocated first to the reservation on the Clear Fork of the Brazos (1855–1859) and then to Oklahoma. Apparently, he died soon after the move north. His name has been said to mean "he pays no attention to happenings," possibly a reference to the dignified detachment that befit an effective chief.

> To reach **Spy's Rock** from **Katemcy Rocks,** continue east on FM 1222 approximately 6 miles to the place where the straightaway road curves southward to round a large solitary hill (Flat Rock); at this point, **Spy's Rock** can be seen just east of due south, at a distance of 1.5 miles.

Spy's (Spice) Rock is remembered in local tradition as a lookout point for hunters from the Comanche bands of Santa Anna and Ketumsee. As an interesting lesson in the corruption of place-names and the loss of their meanings, it is notable that this mound, a place for "spying," is called Spice Rock on some modern maps.

> To reach **Todd Mountain** from **Spy's Rock,** continue east on FM 1222 to the intersection with FM 386; take FM 386 south to the town of Mason; from Mason, take U.S. 87 south about 1.2 miles south of the town center to the RR 1723 fork on the west (right) side of the road, by the roadside park; take RR 1723 south about 2.5 miles and bear west (right) onto RR 2389; take RR 2389 about 0.8 of a mile; **Todd Mountain** is on the south side of the road at the creek crossing.

Judging from its location near trails and an incident recorded in county history, **Todd (Tod) Mountain** was an Indian ambush site. In December 1864, the Todd family (husband, wife, daughter, and a slave girl) was attacked by Comanches at the mountain while traveling to Fort Mason. Mrs. Todd and the slave girl were killed and are buried at the foot of the hill; the Todd's daughter was taken captive and never found.

To reach **Indian Point** from **Todd Mountain,** return to U.S. 87 and head south about 17 miles, to the intersection with FM 783; take FM 783 south about 22 miles, to the community of Doss; from Doss, take FM 648 east about 1 mile; south of this spot lies **Indian Point** at a distance of 0.5 miles.

The scenic cliff of **Indian Point** (Indian Peak) is recorded in local legend as a lookout place for Native scouts. The broad valley unfolding to the north created a passage between the Fredericksburg and Mason areas that served as an alternate to the Pinta Trail. Comanche attacks on settlers were recorded in the area during the 1870s, and pictographs from the prehistoric period were found at a rock shelter within a few miles of this site.

To reach **Cross Mountain** from **Indian Point,** continue east on FM 648 to the intersection with U.S. 87; take U.S. 87 south about 11 miles into the town of Fredericksburg, where the highway becomes Main Street; from the center of town, take FM 965 north, to the edge of town; the first prominent point on the left side of the road, **Cross Mountain,** will be clearly marked by road signs.

Cross Mountain evokes stories about the early interaction between area settlers, who were mostly German, and the Comanches who occupied the region when they arrived. Cross Mountain took its name from a cross erected there by a Spanish missionary, but this priest and the German settlers who followed him co-opted what was originally an Indian signaling point. During the period of settlement, Germans began lighting fires on Cross Mountain and other hills around town every year at Easter time.

At least two plausible explanations for the Easter Fires tradition persist. One reason is that the fires originated as a signal between the Comanches and the settlers that relations were good and a raid was not imminent. Such assurance was desired as the full moon around Easter approached—a favorite Comanche raiding time— even under the successful Meusebach Treaty of 1847.

Another explanation says that the settlers kept many large fires burning around town to make their numbers seem greater and so discourage Indian attacks. The practice may also reflect folk customs from Germany, where bonfires are lit to mark certain seasons. In any case, the settlers found that the fires frightened their children, so they told them that the Easter Bunny made the fires to prepare his Easter eggs. A fire is still lit on Cross Mountain each year on the night before Easter, part of a modern folk pageant that reenacts the story of settlement from the local point of view.

To reach **Enchanted Rock** from **Cross Mountain,** continue north on FM 965 approximately 18 miles; massive domes of pink granite rising 500 feet will loom ahead; follow signs for **Enchanted Rock State Natural Area** to park and explore the site on foot.

There is no more glorious feeling to be had in the Hill Country than when rounding the top of **Enchanted Rock.** Whatever is universally magical about high vistas can be felt abundantly here. And if it is truly possible to feel empathy with Native travelers of the past, this is the place to try. Although Enchanted Rock is constantly associated with Indian reverence and reconnaissance in Anglo lore, there is very little direct evidence of such activities. The famed Hill Country painter Hermann Lungkwitz was compelled to place Indians in the foreground of his 1856 oil of Enchanted Rock, one of several paintings of the site that he composed, but it may have simply been artistic license.

Skeptics of modern attempts to rediscover Indian landmarks, however, are frequently unaware of the rare 1843 pamphlet documenting, in convincing fashion, the captivity of Dolly Webster. The Comanche party holding Webster traveled to Enchanted Rock some time in 1840 and "met with a deputation from several of the Indian nations, who had convened for the purpose of holding a carnival." In the fall of the following year, Texas Ranger Captain John

Enchanted Rock. Photo by Wayne J. Pate

Hays (see **Bandera Pass** and **Uvalde Canyon,** pp. 114–16) was separated from his men and surrounded alone on the summit by Comanches, though he managed to drive them off.

The peculiar pink granite dome emits eerie sounds as the rock expands and contracts with temperature changes, and Anglo lore holds that the nighttime sounds were considered to be spirits by

the Indians. These beliefs may indeed be based on actual knowledge about Indian spirituality: In Comanche religion, unusual hills
like Enchanted Rock were clearly regarded as the abodes of power-
granting spirits, and unusual natural sounds were considered indi-
cations of the presence of spirits.

The Rock, more simply, would have been an ideal location for fast-
ing and praying to achieve spiritual visions. It was also probably a
signaling point. From the top, one can see a number of other promi-
nences across the landscape: Fool Mountain, due east 5.4 miles;
Watch Mountain, 3.3 miles north-northeast; and House Mountain,
8.5 miles to the northwest, which stood just east of the Pinta Trail
(now U.S. 87—see p. 113), a major Indian trail running northwest-
southeast from the San Saba River headwaters to San Antonio.

To reach **Comanche Gap** from **Enchanted Rock,** take FM 965 north
about 9 miles to the intersection with SH 16; take SH 16 north about
17 miles to the town of Llano; from Llano, take SH 29 about 32 miles east
to the town of Burnet; from Burnet, take U.S. 281 about 23.5 miles north
to the town of Lampasas; from Lampasas, take U.S. 190 east about
38 miles through Copperas Cove and Killeen, to Harker Heights;
at Harker Heights, exit U.S. 190 onto FM 2410 going east; proceed
3–4 miles: **Cedar Gap** and then **Comanche Gap** are visible 0.5 miles
south of the roadway; a short detour through **Cedar Gap** is possible
by turning south off FM 2410 onto Comanche Gap Road, which runs
for 3.5 miles and ends at Stillhouse Hollow Lake, Dana Peak Park boat
ramp.

Comanche Gap, and **Cedar Gap** immediately to its west,
allowed passage between the Lampasas River and Nolan Creek
drainages as well as linkage to the main network of Indian trails.
Comanche raiders escaped through this pass in March of 1859 after
killing four settlers and kidnapping two girls; the girls were abandoned in the gap to speed the getaway. It was the last Comanche
raid in Bell County.

To reach **Salado Springs** from **Comanche Gap,** take FM 2410 about
5 miles east to the intersection with U.S. 190; take U.S. 190 east about
5.5 miles to the U.S. 190/IH 35 intersection at Belton; from Belton,

Temporary waterfall at Enchanted Rock. Photo by Wayne J. Pate

take IH 35 about 9 miles to the Salado exit and proceed south to Main Street (FM 2268). Springs emerge in the grove along the south side of Salado Creek just east of where Main Street crosses the creek. The grove can be approached from Royal Street off the east (left) side of Main Street.

For Indian travelers, **Salado Springs** provided a steady supply of cold fresh water, and not saline, as the creek name indicates. The area around the Main Street crossing of Salado Creek was an Indian campground associated with the Tawakonis, though it was probably used by many historic tribes and prehistoric Indians. Like many important Indian water holes, the springs became a stop on a route adopted by non-Indians, in this case the Chisholm Trail made famous during the post–Civil War cattle drives. Wagon wheel ruts from this era can be seen in the creek bedrock around Main Street when the water is low. Salado Springs was Texas's first designated natural landmark.

> To reach **Barton Springs** from **Salado Springs,** continue south on Main Street about 0.8 miles, to the point where it rejoins IH-35 southbound; take IH 35 south about 55 miles to the Riverside Drive intersection on the south side of Austin; Riverside Drive is just south of the IH 35 crossing at Town Lake (Colorado River), but the exit from IH 35 South to Riverside Drive is north of the crossing; take Riverside Drive west about 1 mile to Barton Springs Road; take Barton Springs Road west about 1.5 miles into Zilker Park; **Barton Springs** is within the park on the south side of the road.

Barton Springs is the fourth-largest spring system in Texas. The springs and adjoining Barton Creek—which flows from forty miles west, partly underground—were well known as camping areas for both Tonkawas and Comanches during the 1700s and 1800s. Today the springs supply the famous Barton Springs swimming pool in Zilker Park.

> To reach **San Marcos Springs** from **Barton Springs,** return to IH 35; take IH 35 south about 27 miles to the Loop 82 intersection at San Marcos; take Loop 82 west about 1 mile; Spring Lake formed by San Marcos Springs is on the north (right) side of the road; the springs give rise to the San Marcos River that flows through town and is approachable at many points.

Another Indian watering place adopted by the Spanish and then the Chisholm Trail cattlemen was picturesque **San Marcos Springs,** the second-largest spring system in the state. Ancient occupation here goes back to the Paleo-Indian period, and there is also evidence of late prehistoric gardening at the site. Most interesting is the supposed Tonkawa name recorded for the springs, *Canocanayesatetlo*, said to mean "warm water." After many years as the Aquarena Springs amusement park, the spring lake is now owned by Southwest Texas State University and is slated for more intensive archaeological study.

To reach **Comanche Lookout** from **San Marcos Springs,** continue on Loop 82 about 2 miles beyond Spring Lake, through town, and return to IH 35; take IH 35 south about 32 miles to Loop 1604 (Anderson Loop), on the northern edge of San Antonio; take Loop 1604 west about 2 miles to the Nacogdoches Road intersection; take Nacogdoches Road south about 1.4 miles; **Comanche Lookout** and city park entrance are on the west side of the road; parking to explore the site on foot is available at the park.

Like many of the key lookout posts, **Comanche Lookout (Comanche Hill)** appears much more prominent from some directions than others. Viewed from the northwest where Loop 1604 swings by, the summit is hardly more noticeable than those around it, except that you may spot the top of the masonry castle tower near the crown of the hill rising above the treetops. A better sense of elevation is gained by approaching the hill from the south along Nacogdoches Road, but even without climbing the tower, viewers can command a wide sweep of the country to the north and east from the top of the hill. At this point, they can see where the Spanish colonial traffic between San Antonio de Béxar and Nacogdoches once ran—the Camino Real, or Royal Road. This is the highest spot in northeast San Antonio and the fourth-highest elevation in the entirety of Bexar County. The English chronicler of Texas in the 1830s, William Bollaert, called the hill "Indian Lookout" and noted that both Indians and whites used it to watch over the Camino Real.

An archaeological survey conducted by the University of Texas at San Antonio in 1997 noted natural outcrops of chert as well as evidence of prehistoric Indian occupation on the upper slopes of

San Pedro Springs. Photo by Daniel J. Gelo

the Lookout. The stone tower was built between 1923 and 1948 by a former landowner, Colonel Edward Coppock. With a tinge of irony, it may be noted that Colonel Coppock retired to the spot after forty-four years of service in the U.S. Army, including fighting the Sioux and Apaches; in addition, he modeled his tower after one built by William the Conqueror. After many years of neglect, the property has been turned into a city park.

To reach **San Pedro Springs** from **Comanche Lookout,** return north on Nacogdoches Road to Loop 1604; take Loop 1604 east about 2 miles to the IH 35 intersection; take IH 35 south about 16 miles to the San Pedro intersection; take San Pedro north about 1 mile north to Ashby Avenue; turn west (left) on Ashby Avenue; the park entrance is on the left; park by the San Pedro Playhouse and follow the sidewalk south to approach the springs on foot.

San Pedro Springs in San Pedro Park, a famous Indian landmark and one of the headwaters of the San Antonio River, was also the foundation of Spanish settlement in San Antonio. In addition to the main springs at the head of the park swimming pool, several others bubble up around the park lawn to the southeast during wetter periods. Likely known to all the tribes, San Pedro Springs was the location of an encampment of people called Payayas, who were probably Coahuiltecan speakers, in the 1690s. Their name for the San Antonio River (or some place along it) was *Yanaguana*, and it is the only word in their language, other than their name, that has been preserved for modern times. It has been said to mean "refreshing waters," though this meaning may be a modern invention.

In 1709, the Spanish recorded other Coahuiltecans camped at the San Antonio headwaters, members of the bands called Sipuans (Chayopins), Chaulaames (Sulijames), and Sijames. All of these groups ranged from the South Texas brush country into the southern reaches of the Edwards Plateau. When seen on the upper San Antonio River, they were probably clustering off the path of the Apaches who had in recent times begun dominating the northern part of their traditional territory. Within two decades, they would find better refuge in the missions and begin assimilating into the general Hispanic society of South Texas. Later, Comanches approaching San Antonio to negotiate with the Spanish used San Pedro Springs as a focal point.

To reach the **Chihuahua Trail** from **San Pedro Springs,** return to IH 35 and proceed south about 3.5 miles to the U.S. 90 intersection; take U.S. 90 about 4.7 miles to the place where Castroville Road and Acme intersect immediately north of U.S. 90; take Castroville Road east of this location and then U.S. 90 west of this location to follow the **Chihuahua Trail.**

The **Chihuahua Trail** was a well-worn pathway for Apache and Comanche travelers and probably the Jumanos before them. It was the forerunner of Castroville Road, leading west out of San Antonio, and its successor, modern U.S. 90, which joins San Antonio, Castroville, and Uvalde. The Chihuahua Trail tied into the system sometimes called the Comanche War Trail, including the path through Horsehead Crossing on the Pecos River and

Water hole at San Pedro Springs. Photo by Daniel J. Gelo

Presidio in Big Bend, and from Big Bend into northern Mexico (see chapter 7).

To reach **Paso de Los Apaches** from the **Chihuahua Trail**, continue on U.S. 90 about 4 miles to the Loop 410 intersection; take Loop 410 north and east about 12.5 miles to the IH 10 intersection;

> take IH 10 west (north) about 8 miles to the Loop 1604 intersection;
> **Paso de Los Apaches** begins along IH 10 about 1 mile beyond this
> intersection.

The area that resembles a small mountain pass just northwest of
the IH 10–Loop 1604 intersection, actually an entrance into the Balcones Escarpment, is the gap noted in various early records as **Paso
de Los Apaches** (Apache Pass) or **Puerta Pinta** (Paint Pass). This
may also be the gap that the Swiss botanist Jean Louis Berlandier
referred to as **Puerto Viejo** (Old Pass), and the one called **Puerto
de Los Payayas** (Payaya Pass) by Miranda in 1756. Somewhere in
the vicinity too was the spring that Berlandier called Ojo de Agua—
literally "eye of water," a generic Spanish term for *spring*—perhaps
Leon Springs just west of the highway at the exit by that name, or
Comanche Springs on the Camp Bullis Military Reserve east of the
highway. This area was the escarpment entranceway to the **Pinta
Trail** that connected San Antonio with the headwaters of the San
Saba River near Menard.

Lipan Apaches and later Comanches made use of the trail in
their movements during war and peace. Spanish forces pursued
the Apaches along this route in the 1700s, and Berlandier rode
the trace with fellow explorers and fifty or more Comanches on a
hunting trip in November 1828. Segments of the trail were later
used by German wagoneers, 49ers, and army troops, but use faded
when the railroads were built in the late 1800s (again, more or less
along the same path). Modern roads take advantage of some of the
same grades and mountain gaps.

At Paso de Los Apaches, the trail ran parallel to Cibolo Creek,
which lies east of present IH 10. The trail followed the present IH
10 corridor before turning due north to cross the Guadalupe River
near Waring or Sisterdale—there may have been multiple prongs of
the trail through the hills here—along RR 1379 or Old San Antonio
Road. Then the trail took a jog west on present U.S. 290, through
Main Street in Fredericksburg, and north again along present U.S.
87. At West Comanche Creek, just northwest of Mason, the trail
turned west from present U.S. 87 toward Menard, corresponding
to present SH 29.

At this point, either the Hill Country tour can be brought to full circle by returning to Menard via the roads just outlined, or more sites can be visited by proceeding next to **Helotes.**

To reach **Helotes** from **Paso de Los Apaches,** continue on IH 10 about 6 miles beyond the IH 10–Loop 1604 intersection to the Boerne Stage Road intersection at Leon Springs; take Boerne Stage Road west about 3 miles to the intersection with Scenic Loop Road; take Scenic Loop Road south about 8 miles, through Grey Forest to the intersection with SH 16 (Bandera Road) at **Helotes.**

Local tradition holds that Apache Indians, presumably Lipans, were occupying the small canyons around **Helotes** when Euro-Americans settled the village in the 1850s.

To reach **Bandera Pass** from **Helotes,** take SH 16 west (north) about 33 miles to the intersection with FM 173 on the north (right) side of the road in the town of Bandera; take FM 173 north about 13 miles; you will enter **Bandera Pass** just south of the Bandera-Kerr County line.

The hills around the headwaters of the Guadalupe and Medina Rivers were famous as Indian reconnaissance and smoke-signaling points. Also, the Medina River banks around Bandera were reputedly the source of mineral pigments that Indian people traveled great distances to obtain. It is no wonder, then, that the most strategic gorge in the area, **Bandera Pass,** became the site of not one but two notorious encounters, as well as several minor skirmishes.

Early in the 1700s, a Spanish patrol out of San Antonio engaged a band of Apaches in a three-day battle in the pass. It may have been during this era that the site received its name, which is Spanish for "flag." A Spanish map from around 1810 shows an Apache village just north of the gap. Swiss botanist Jean Louis Berlandier, exploring with a Mexican government survey party from 1828 to 1829, tells us:

Here a Comanche warrior is buried, and since the natives often pass this way, every tribe that passes close enough to see the grave of one of their ancestors makes the customary offerings. On the grave they place arrows, bows, sundry weapons, enemy trophies, and the like, and even sacrifice mules and horses to his shade. The gorge, which is widely known for this custom, is strewn with the bones of the animals that have been sacrificed there. The grave itself is surrounded by skulls.

When Anglos occupied the area and began concerted attempts to control Indian movements, the path through the pass became part of the Old Texas Ranger Trail, linking the Medina and Guadalupe Rivers; the U.S. Army later used the route to connect frontier forts. In 1841, some forty Texas Rangers under Indian fighter Jack Hays were ambushed midway through the pass by a large force of Comanches who had lain hidden amid the rocks and brush. The rangers fought a bloody hand-to-hand action, much of it with Bowie knives. It is said that the Indians withdrew upon the death of their leader, which may well be true since Plains warriors often gave up to fight another day once the raid organizer was killed.

To reach **Uvalde Canyon** from **Bandera Pass,** return south on FM 173 to the SH 16 intersection in the town of Bandera; take SH 16 north about 2.5 miles to the intersection with SH 470 on west (left) side of road; take SH 470 about 33 miles, through Tarpley to the intersection with SH 187 north of Utopia; take SH 187 south about 26 miles to the U.S. 90 intersection at Sabinal.

The north-south river courses through the southern hills of the Edwards Plateau were natural highways for Native people. The most famous of these passages was the Sabinal River canyon, formerly known as **Uvalde Canyon.** The canyon, as well as the town of Uvalde to the southwest, preserves the corrupted name of Juan de Ugalde, the Spanish *comandante de armas* who shaped Indian policy and campaigned against the Apaches in the 1780s. Ugalde forged an alliance of Comanches and Wichitas to route the Apaches in a battle at the site of present Utopia.

Comanches then fell heir to the region, as early Spanish maps show a "Comanche Trail" corresponding to the present road along the river. Jack Hays and Juan Seguin led a posse into the canyon in June 1839 and destroyed recently abandoned Comanche villages. Comanche spokesmen in 1844 treaty negotiations mentioned Uvalde Canyon as the southwesternmost point on an imaginary boundary running along the Balcones Escarpment, the border of what they considered vital buffalo-hunting territory. In the early 1870s, the canyon probably served as the launching place for the numerous raids made in the area by Apaches and Kickapoos, who by that time dwelled mainly in northern Mexico.

To reach **Chalk Bluff** from **Uvalde Canyon,** take U.S. 90 west about 25 miles to the U.S. 83 (Greer Street) intersection at Uvalde; take U.S. 83 north 2 miles, just beyond the railroad overpass, to the intersection with SH 55 on the west (left) side of the road; take SH 55 northwest about 15 miles to the road marked "Park Chalk Bluff" on the west (left) side of the road; proceed on the road about 1 mile to Park Chalk Bluff campground. The camp is open for day visits from 8:30 A.M. to 8:30 P.M. in summer, 8:30 A.M. till dark in winter. Day visitors are charged a small fee. Reservations are recommended for overnight camping; call (830) 278-5515.

Chalk Bluff is just visible from the highway, but a detour is well worth it for a quick visit, a day of picnicking, or overnight camping. The white cave-ridden bluff rising 350 feet for 2.5 miles along the pristine Nueces River is a true natural wonder. While there seem to be no eyewitness accounts or tribal traditions about Indian ritualism at this site, it is very likely that vision quests were held here. Chalk Bluff is quite similar in appearance to Medicine Bluffs north of Lawton, Oklahoma, which has been well documented as a ceremonial site for the Kiowas and Comanches (see chapter 5). It is also an ideal campsite, with fine water and with cliffs sheltering campers from prevailing west winds.

It is established that much Indian traffic went past this site, so non-Indian intruders were probably particularly unwelcome here. On May 29, 1861, renowned Indian fighters Henry Robinson and Henry Adams were ambushed and killed at Chalk Bluff by Indians of an unidentified tribe. Robinson had worked out of Fort Inge (4.5 miles southeast of Uvalde) and become so well known to the Indians, all the more because of his red beard, that it is said they made a pictograph of his image on a rock near the Llano River. Adams, from Potranco Creek near San Antonio, was Robinson's daughter's fiancé.

The men were on their way to Camp Wood and had stopped by the bluff to make coffee when the attack came. The attackers, who numbered sixteen or twenty according to different accounts, crept along under cover of some driftwood and killed the men before they could reach their guns. After taking the scalps and Robinson's beard, too, the warriors went on to attack Robinson's house seven miles away. Mrs. Robinson defended her children by throwing rocks. The Indians, probably out of respect for her bravery, spared most of the family. They did, however, ransack the house. Placing a portrait of Robinson on the floor, they laid a sock they had stripped from his body ceremoniously across his image.

To reach **West Nueces Canyon** from **Chalk Bluff,** return to SH 55 and proceed north about 5 miles to the intersection with SH 334 on the west (left) side of the road at Laguna; take SH 334 west about 34 miles to the intersection with SH 674 at Brackettville; this road follows the canyon.

The **West Nueces Canyon** was a remote and secure camping area known to Comanche and Kiowa expeditions; it was likely used by Kickapoos and other groups as well. According to U.S. Army records, a small valley off this canyon was the headquarters for a Comanche and Kiowa raid into Mexico in December 1873.

To reach **Las Moras Springs** from **West Nueces Canyon,** take SH 674 south about 1 mile to the intersection with U.S. 90; proceed on U.S. 90 east less than 0.1 mile to Bowie Road, which is the entrance to the Fort Clarke Springs private resort community on the south (right) side of highway; take Bowie Road a short distance to Swim Park Lane on the west (right) side of the road; follow Swim Park Lane about 0.6 miles to view **Las Moras Springs.**

The ninth-largest spring system in the state, **Las Moras Springs** served prehistoric and historic Indians as well as Spanish colonists traveling between El Paso and San Antonio. In 1840, cavalry drove off Comanches camping at the springs. Lieutenant William Henry Chase Whiting rediscovered the springs in 1849 while exploring an east-west route for the U.S. Army Corps of Engineers. Whiting wrote in his journal that the springs were hidden in a dense grove of pecans and mulberries, and he noted as a landmark Las Moras Mountain rising to the northeast at a distance of about 3.5 miles:

> About three miles off stands the hill, a remarkable feature of the country. It is of no great elevation, not being higher than the table formation farther to the north, but it rises solitary with its two eminences from the midst of a beautiful plain of great extent. It is a favorite lookout of the Indians, and many trails for Mexican depredation come by this point from the upper Nueces, the Llano, and the San Saba. (Bieber and Bender 1938, p. 348)

Fort Clark was established here in 1852 as the southernmost in a line of forts intended to monitor Indian traffic and guard settlers; it remained an active post until 1944. At Fort Clark were stationed many of the Black Seminole scouts recruited to guide the army campaigns against the Kickapoos, Comanches, and Kiowas in the 1870s (see **Seminole Draw,** chapter 6, p. 156). These were largely former African American slaves of Seminole Indians in Florida including their mixed-blood descendants who had been relocated in Oklahoma, Texas, and Mexico. As brave trackers and fighters familiar with English, Spanish, and multiple Indian languages, they provided effective service in the borderlands. The Black Seminoles attached to Fort Clark lived in Seminole Camp along Las Moras Creek south of the springs when they were not out on patrol. After the scout units were disbanded in 1912, they moved into Brackettville and maintained a community that still exists.

To reach a view of the **Anacacho Mountains** from **Las Moras Springs,** take U.S. 90 east about 18.5 miles; the mountains are about 1 mile south of the roadway at this point.

As a sheltering area at the juncture of different tribal zones of influence, the **Anacacho Mountains** long functioned as a meeting and trading place as well as a campsite available to numerous groups. Prehistoric traders probably camped here on a customary route between the Puebloan settlements of the Rio Grande and Caddoan East Texas. When the Apaches pushed southward and eastward through the Hill Country through the 1600s, they disrupted Jumanos, Tonkawas, Coahuiltecans, and various groups from northern Mexico, who gathered at this location.

The Frenchman Juan Jarri (or Jarry; probably Jean Géry), a deserter from the 1685 La Salle Expedition, may have lived here as the leader of a Coahuiltecan village for some years before being captured by Spaniards fearful of French intrusion; one authority places Jarri's village a little further north, on the escarpment. Spanish records give another name for the range, Sierra Decate, based on an Indian name of unknown origin.

To complete a full circuit for the Hill Country route, proceed 21 miles back to Uvalde, to the intersection with U.S. 83 (Greer Street); take U.S. 83 north about 128 miles to Menard.

5

THE ROLLING PLAINS

B etween the picturesque Hill Country and the stark, high table of the Staked Plains, there lies an intermediate zone of prairies and badlands that formerly hosted a great deal of Indian activity: the Rolling Plains. It was an area "abounding with numerous clear spring branches for two hundred miles," with a climate "salubrious and healthy," the explorer and U.S. Army Captain Randolph Marcy trumpeted in 1849. The region actually extends well into Oklahoma, serving as a zone of mobility for Indian travelers between the mountains and river valleys and destinations in Texas and Mexico.

To the south and east, the Rolling Plains merge into the Hill Country terrain of Central Texas, and they also yield to the East Texas piney woods. The abundance of springwater noted by Marcy is no longer so much in evidence because, as elsewhere in the state, the water table has been drawn down by human activity. Yet, many of the key landmarks and camping places of Indian days still remain for the knowledgeable visitor to view.

At the dawn of the historic period, the Rolling Plains would have served as an excellent north-south route for the Jumanos moving north from the Rio Grande settlements. As these celebrated traders traveled to connect the eastern forest dwellers with the Pueblos of the western deserts, the Rolling Plains would again have provided them with comfortable camping and ensured food and water.

The relative ease of travel afforded by the region made the Apache invasion of Texas that much easier; the Comanches, Cheyennes, and Kiowas who followed them also chose the Rolling Plains as a pathway. Yet, farming tribes found the area hospitable as well, at least after they were displaced from the more desirable locations to the east. The different subtribes of Wichita Indians in particular chose to locate on the rivers of the Rolling Plains around the period 1834–1845, as white-settlement pressure mounted to the east.

The Wacos, Tawakonis, and Kichais set up their villages of beehive-like grass lodges at the junction of Wichita Creek and Red River (modern Wichita Falls), as well as on the Trinity and Brazos west of Dallas–Fort Worth. Members of fugitive semisedentary tribes from the northeast, including the Delawares, Shawnees, and Kickapoos, also ventured into the area around this time and stayed for several years; distant raiders such as the Osages and Pawnees rode through as well. The first Comanche reservation, involving members of the southernmost Penateka band, was established in 1855 on the Clear Fork of the Brazos in Throckmorton County. It was an experiment in converting the horse Indians into farmers, but it lasted only four years, disrupted by Comanches from other bands and by aggressive, advancing settlers.

At once a pathway and marginal homeland, the region has long been contested ground among Indian tribes and between Indians and whites. The last Comanche raid in Texas occurred in 1879 near Big Spring. It was four years since the last tribe members had surrendered and come in to the subsequent reservation in Oklahoma, at the foot of the Wichita Mountains. Some young men, seeking a taste of the traditional glory they no longer would regularly enjoy, sneaked away and rode, one last time, down the Rolling Plains.

THE LAY OF THE LAND

The Rolling Plains forms the part of the Great Plains physiographic province extending from the Canadian River in Oklahoma to the

The Rolling Plains

Sites

1. Santa Anna Peaks
2. Pecan Bayou
3. Buffalo Gap
4. Abilene State Park
5. Sanco
6. Squaretop Mt.
7. Gunsight Mts.
8. Mushaway Peak
9. Bull Creek Canyon
10. Courthouse Mountain
11. Blanco Canyon/Silver Falls
12. Quitaque Peaks
13. Tee Pee City
14. Double Mountain
15. Kiowa Peak
16. Medicine Mounds
17. Brushy Mound
18. Queens Peak
19. Spanish Fort
20. Devil's Backbone
21. Jim Ned Lookout
22. Comanche Peak
23. Boys Peak

Cities and Towns

A. Santa Anna
B. Coleman
C. Buffalo Gap
D. Bronte
E. Robert Lee
F. Sanco
G. Sterling City
H. Big Spring
I. Vealmore
J. Gail
K. Post
L. Ralls

M. Crosbyton
N. Floydada
O. Flomot
P. Matador
Q. Roaring Springs
R. Dickens
S. Spur
T. Jayton
U. Aspermont
V. Old Glory
W. Rule
X. O'Brien
Y. Knox City
Z. Benjamin
AA. Crowell
BB. Quanah
CC. Chillicothe
DD. Vernon
EE. Electra
FF. Iowa Park
GG. Wichita Falls
HH. Henrietta
II. Bellevue
JJ. Bowie
KK. Stoneburg
LL. Montague
MM. Nocona
NN. Spanish Fort
OO. Saint Jo
PP. Forestburg
QQ. Alvord
RR. Decatur
SS. Springtown
TT. Weatherford
UU. Granbury
VV. Glen Rose
WW. Chalk Mt.
XX. Hico
YY. Hamilton
ZZ. Lampasas

Texas Hill Country, and from the Llano Estacado on the west to the East Texas prairies and woods. Unlike the flat Staked Plains, this area is indeed generally undulating, although it contains some level stretches.

It is easy here to sense the gigantic geological forces that have been at work for ages; in essence, the Rolling Plains is the more broken, irregular fringe of the Great Plains—broken through erosion caused by both the runoff from the higher plains and the somewhat greater rainfall that occurs here as compared to the High Plains. The erosive scarring of the landscape is noticeable in the irregular mounds and buttes that have remained while their surroundings washed away, as well as in the narrow but deep drainages that cut through the soil surface. These creek beds are referred to locally as "breaks," or "copper breaks," since some reveal layers containing this metal.

Reddish brown and gray brown loams form a topsoil layer a half-foot thick, except on areas of rocky outcrops where a thinner layer of sandy loam is evident. Further down lies a variety of bedrocks such as gypsum and sandstone. In general, the geologic materials of the region date to the Permian period, 220 to 285 million years ago, although some soil types were introduced by wind action much later, in the Quarternary period (starting 1.8 million years ago).

The rain that sculpts the landscape comes mainly in thundershowers, which in their frequency or seasonal appearance are never predictable. Annual rainfall amounts vary widely around the long-term average of twenty-five inches per year. Summers are usually dry and hot, winters dry and cool, with periodic vicious winter winds and gloomy skies when the northers blow through. The cold spells occur consistently and predictably as the winter wears on. Thus, one rancher said of the Fort Worth Fat Stock Show and Rodeo held in February: "Hell, we don't even check the calendar—we just wait till the weather turns really ugly, then we load up and go!" It snows rarely, however, less frequently here than in the higher elevation of the Staked Plains to the west. The general climate is therefore intermediate between that of the dry High Plains and humid East Texas.

The east-flowing streams of the region still gather sufficient water to provide good locations for campsites and settlements even during dry seasons. An excellent example of Indian use of the Rolling Plains streams is found in the journal of a north-south trip made in the spring of 1875 by the Comanche chief Wild Horse and J. J. Sturm, the post interpreter from Fort Sill. Nearly every night, they were able to camp by good water along the various tributaries of the Red, Brazos, and Colorado Rivers. The Rolling Plains streams all had descriptive Comanche names that have been recorded on early Texas maps, such as the map published by Stephen F. Austin in 1836.

For vegetation, the Rolling Plains is a transition zone. Plains grass species of both mid- and short height are found, including buffalo grass, bluestem, grama, and three-awn. The grasses may form dense sods or dispersed bunches depending on local conditions. In many places, mesquites, cactuses, junipers, and thorny shrubs create a thin and more or less continuous overstory. Stands of woody vegetation are found here and there, especially along creeks and scarps. Trees and shrubs in these areas, in addition to the ones mentioned, may include cottonwood, willows, hackberry, china, oak, sumac, and sand plum. Although this ground cover may appear minimal to someone used to forested land, it actually harbors a rich variety of animal life. Smaller mammals abound—possums, raccoons, ground squirrels, gophers, and kangaroo rats. Bobcats and coyotes are common predators, once joined by timber wolves and mountain lions.

The most notable animal occupants from the Indian viewpoint were the large grass eaters: deer, antelope, and bison. Healthy populations of white-tailed and mule deer remain. Antelope are scarce, however, and the buffalo are now gone—except those that can be seen on private ranches or in the Wichita Mountains Wildlife Refuge near Lawton, Oklahoma. The abundant grass of the open areas, plus the shelter and forage offered in the breaks, made the Rolling Plains a fine place to hunt the large-hoofed animals, especially when they broke into small groups for the winter.

Apart from the woods found along creek bottoms, a most remarkable large woodland zone runs in two parallel prongs from north to south through the middle of the Rolling Plains, between the ninety-sixth and ninety-ninth meridians. The Cross Timbers may have been so called because the streams of the plains had to cross through them or because they stood perpendicular to the westward routes of settlers. These dense stands of blackjack oak and post oak that extend from southern Kansas, across Oklahoma, and into North Texas were so troublesome to Anglo travelers that the writer Washington Irving referred to them as the "Cast Iron Forest."

For Indian people, the Cross Timbers were a mixed blessing. The zone was sometimes an avenue for north-south passage, but the secrecy it provided was offset by the difficulty of travel it presented. Sedentary farmers such as the Wichitas apparently enjoyed the protection and the plentiful supply of wood that the Cross Timbers offered, but the thick vegetation hampered any Indians on horseback.

Although some writers have suggested that the Comanche band names Hois (Timber People) or Penateka (Honey Eaters) indicated an association with the Cross Timber country, the woods were a natural boundary that the Comanches seldom passed; they were, in effect, the dividing line between the hunting grounds of the East and West Texas tribes. Remnants of the Cross Timbers can be seen in several Texas locations between the Red River and Waco.

Moving through the region from east to west, the traveler will notice at least three gradual changes. First, the population thins, and towns are located farther apart toward the west. Second, apart from the Cross Timbers, breaks, and badlands that are encountered, the terrain flattens out and broadens, providing more extensive vistas. Cattle ranching and farming are also increasingly dominant toward the west. But perhaps the most important realization a traveler will have is an impression of the entire area, and it is a feeling that is anticlimactic.

Unlike the High Plains or the West Texas mountains and basins, which in places suggest every movie fan's image of the wild frontier, the Rolling Plains does not present a powerful picture of "Indian Country." The area is at least equally suggestive of the farmer and rancher's West, tamed and productive in the modern sense. Here we see the vision posed by the Indian fighter General Phil Sheridan, in his famous speech before the 1875 Texas legislature urging the eradication of the buffalo:

> [The buffalo hunters] are destroying the Indian's commissary; and it is a well-known fact that an army losing its base of supplies is placed at a great disadvantage. Send them powder and lead, if you will; but, for the sake of lasting peace, let them kill, skin, and sell until the buffaloes are exterminated. Then your prairies can be covered with speckled cattle, and the festive cowboy, who follows the hunter as a second forerunner of an advanced civilization. (Quoted in Cook 1989, p. 113)

EXPLORING THE ROLLING PLAINS

The journey around the Rolling Plains begins at **Santa Anna Peaks,** at the town of Santa Anna in east-central Coleman County. **Santa Anna Peaks** will come into view from 12 miles to the south on U.S. 283. Continue to the U.S. 283/U.S. 84 intersection at the foot of the peaks, and take U.S. 283/84 west and north around the western end of the mountains. The best view of the whole formation is obtained from the northwest, at the roadside picnic area about 3 miles past the U.S. 283/U.S. 84 intersection.

Santa Anna Peaks is one of only a few places in the state that takes its name from a known Comanche person. Santa Anna (?–1849) was a leader of the Penateka, or southern band of Comanches, who occupied Central Texas during the early 1800s. He was an influential warrior and diplomat who shaped Indian–white relations during the period, leading resistance against Anglo settlers until he visited Washington, D.C. (he was the first Comanche leader to do so). After which, impressed by the scale of the advancing civilization, he sought ways to establish peace. Santa Anna reportedly took his recorded name after the infamous Mexican general at the Alamo massacre. He died in the devastating cholera epidemic brought by the 49ers passing through Texas.

Santa Anna Peaks. Photo by Daniel J. Gelo

Santa Anna's followers frequently camped on and around the mesa, which has been reduced and reshaped to some extent by quarrying over the last decades. Still, by approaching from the south, one gets a clear sense of the looming grandeur of this formation and the way Indian sentinels could have commanded a wide view from the top. As the highway turns west through the town of Santa Anna and then swings northwest again, the roadway climbs along the flank of the mesa; look here for a place to pull over, either at the rest area or further along the road, and gaze out to the west. On a clear day, you'll see Bead Mountain 14.5 miles distant, no doubt another link in a chain of smoke-signaling sites.

To reach **Pecan Bayou** from **Santa Anna Peaks,** continue north from the roadside picnic area on U.S. 283 for about 32 miles, to a point just beyond where the road curves from due north to northeast, or less than 2 miles south of the U.S. 283/SH 36 intersection; at this point, the road crosses **Pecan Bayou.**

Pecan Bayou has been noted as the westernmost of all the bodies of water called "bayou." A glimpse at this location will show the heavy vegetation that runs all along the creek and includes many pecan trees. These trees were an attraction for the Indian people of several tribes in the historic period because pecan nuts are very rich in fat, which was otherwise relatively scarce in the diets of hunter–gatherers. Band members would congregate along Pecan Bayou for several days to enjoy the harvest.

To reach **Buffalo Gap** from **Pecan Bayou,** continue north on U.S. 283 about 1.7 miles to the SH 36 intersection; take SH 36 west about 16 miles to the FM 1705 intersection on the west (left) side of the road; take FM 1705 north (west and north) about 6.5 miles to the FM 707 intersection on the west (left) side of the road; take FM 707 west about 4.7 miles, to the SH 89 intersection; take SH 89 south about 6.4 miles to the intersection with SH 613 at the community of Buffalo Gap; you have just passed through **Buffalo Gap,** for which the town is named.

Buffalo Gap and Cedar Gap to the east both cut through the Callahan Divide, the range of hills separating the Brazos and Colorado River watersheds. The section of the divide in between the gaps is known as Steamboat Mountain. Buffalo Gap has better water than Cedar Gap, in the form of Elm Creek, and it opens southward into a huge natural amphitheater that was a great buffalo grazing ground in the old days. The gap itself was a natural funnel that forced herding bison into a more manageable target for Indian hunters. Plains Indians customarily drove buffalo through ravines when pursuing them so that the herd would line up. Individual animals were thus easier to ride up on, and the Indians knew to congregate at Buffalo Gap for this effective procedure.

Their continuing visits made the gap a natural place for the growth of trade and, eventually, for white buffalo hunting and settlement. In his memoirs, Herman Lehmann, a captive German boy from Fredericksburg who rode willingly with Apache and Comanche raiders in the mid-1800s, supposed Buffalo Gap to be the scene of a close call he and his companions faced many years earlier:

> We were going through a pass in the mountains, possibly it was Buffalo Gap, and ran right into a camp of white men before we saw them. Realizing that we had to act promptly we put our herd into a run and went through the camp yelling and shooting. It was just at daylight, and the sleeping men arose as one man and made a break for the brush, not taking time to get their guns. As we went through we picked up two of their horses and carried them along, but we did not tarry to find out how many men were in the camp, and as they did not follow us we made a safe get-away. We soon struck the buffalo trails, which insured obliteration of our herd trail, and reached our village with a good bunch of horses. (Lehmann 1993, p. 166)

Be sure to visit Buffalo Gap Historic Village, a complex of twenty restored frontier buildings, with excellent interpretations and exhibits, including Indian artifacts. For admission and information, phone (915) 572-3365.

To reach **Abilene State Park** from **Buffalo Gap,** continue south on SH 89 by bearing west (right) at the SH 89/SH 613 intersection and proceed about 4.2 miles to the Park Road 32 intersection on the east (left) side of the road; enter here for **Abilene State Park.**

The enormous pecan grove along Elm Creek at **Abilene State Park** was used as a camping place by Tonkowas and Comanches, and possibly other tribes, during their hunts around Buffalo Gap.

To reach **Sanco** from **Abilene State Park,** return to SH 89 and proceed south (west) about 7 miles to the U.S. 277 intersection; take U.S. 277 south about 34 miles, to the SH 158 intersection at Bronte; take SH 158 west about 12 miles to the U.S. 208 intersection at Robert Lee; take U.S. 208 about 6.3 miles to the blacktop county road on the north (right) side of the highway, marked "Sanco Loop"; take Sanco Loop about 2.7 miles to the community of **Sanco.**

Sanco is another of the very few places that preserve the name of a known Comanche leader. *Sanaco* is the usual spelling of the name of a celebrated Penateka Comanche chief who lived in the mid-1800s. His name has often been translated as "chewing gum," which probably refers to the sap of the slippery elm tree that Indians chewed to enjoy the flavor and to slake their thirst while traveling.

Sanaco rivaled fellow Penateka leaders Buffalo Hump and Ketumsee, offering his followers a more hard-line approach to dealing with white settlers. It is said that Texans killed his father in the infamous 1840 Council House fight in San Antonio. Though he could be a skillful negotiator, Sanaco often opted for either raiding or avoidance. His band, like the other Penateka groups, was ravaged by cholera and smallpox in 1849.

After the Penatekas were located on the Clear Fork Reserve in 1854, Sanaco led a large proportion of them away from the reservation in dissatisfaction, weakening government efforts to settle the Indians and undermining Ketumsee's leadership. The stretch of Yellow Wolf Creek at the present site of the Sanco community was one of the favorite camping places for Sanaco and his followers prior to 1854; they are also placed elsewhere along the Colorado and San Saba Rivers at various times in the historical record. Strangely, Yellow Wolf was another Penateka leader from the same period, and he is commemorated by the creek name—perhaps he also used the campsite or was buried in the area.

To reach **Squaretop Mountain** from **Sanco,** return east on Sanco Loop about 0.2 miles to the unimproved county road leading east-southeast from Sanco; take the unimproved road about 2 miles; at this point, less than a half-mile northeast of the road, **Squaretop Mountain** rises about 400 feet.

Squaretop Mountain is known locally as a place of Indian activity. Although the shape of the hilltop more closely resembles a triangle when viewed from the northwest, it looks square from the opposite direction. Its dominance of the surrounding area and position at the southwest end of a scattering of prominent hills made it ideal as a lookout and a signaling point; it covers a major stretch of the broad and shallow Colorado River Valley that meanders about ten miles to the south. The Colorado River Valley was a

East and West Gunsight Mountains. Photo by Wayne J. Pate

major thoroughfare of Indian travel and a component of the Eastern Comanche Trace.

To reach **Gunsight Mountains** from **Squaretop Mountain,** return west-northwest to Sanco; take Sanco Loop south (left) to the SH 208 intersection; return south (left) on SH 208 to the SH 158 intersection at Robert Lee; take SH 158 west about 35 miles to the U.S. 87 intersection at Sterling City; take U.S. 87 north (west) about 52 miles, through Big Spring, and past the IH 20 intersection to the FM 1584 intersection on the east (right) side of the highway; take FM 1584 north about 11.5 miles to FM 1584/FM 1785, the intersection at Vealmore (if you reach the Borden County line on FM 1584, you have gone too far); take FM 1785 east about 6.6 miles, past FM 669 and through two curves; toward the end of the second curve, **West Gunsight Mountain** will be visible about 1.4 miles to the south (right), and **East Gunsight Mountain** will be visible almost straight ahead, at a distance of about 2 miles.

Though neither landmark would qualify as a mountain to anyone except a native of West Texas, both **East and West Gunsight Mountains** do resemble gun sights. The east mountain is flat on top, with a notch in the middle just like the rear sight on most rifles and pistols; the west mountain, smaller and flat across the top, looks like the rear sight on early military rifles. Both features also appear to rise above the surrounding terrain about as much as a gun sight rises above a gun barrel.

Other hills in Texas are called "Gunsight," but these two in particular deserve the name: The gap between them marks a straight, near-perfect path between the landmarks of Mushaway Peak to the north (see below) and Big Spring twenty miles to the south, which is the great water hole and nexus of Indian trails and which is also itself marked by two hills that in effect echo the dual aspect of the Gunsights (see chapter 6).Though no historical references have yet been found to Indian use of the East and West Gunsights, such use seems highly likely owing to their exact position between two well-known Indian destinations.

To reach **Mushaway Peak** from the **Gunsight Mountains,** continue east on FM 1785 about 5 miles to the FM 1785/Willow Valley Road intersection—Willow Valley Road is a paved county road running only to the north (left); take Willow Valley Road about 10 miles, beyond the Colorado River; **Mushaway Peak** will come into view to the northeast (right). The best view is from a depression in the roadway. Note how the elevation of the peak seems to lessen as the road climbs.

The modern name **Mushaway Peak** preserves one of the few Comanche terms in modern Texas geography. Another English variant is Muchuquay, closer to the original *motso ku?e,* "beard summit." (Note: the question mark is a conventional way of representing a particular sound [glottal stop] in the Comanche language.) In 1874, Comanche guides told Fort Sill post interpreter J. J. Sturm that the name referred to the tribal legend of an old man who sat on the hill plucking his beard (Comanches liked to remove their scant facial hair with mussel shell tweezers).

Though a curiosity in and of itself and therefore a good rendezvous site, Mushaway Peak was also used as a navigation aid for

Mushaway Peak in melting snow. Photo by Wayne J. Pate

Comanches traveling north-south on the Rolling Plains to skirt the Llano Estacado escarpment. By turning west from the peak, they would encounter the openings to key camping and hiding places—that is, the canyons piercing the east face of the escarpment. From lookout spots on the escarpment above these canyons, Mushaway is easily seen on the horizon, which suggests that it could have been a signaling place for contacting tribe mates seeking refuge in the canyons.

To reach a distant view of **Bull Creek Canyon** from **Mushaway Peak,** continue north on Willow Valley Road about 6.5 miles, past the U.S. 180 intersection at Gail, to the SH 669 intersection; take SH 669 north about 12 miles, or about 6 miles past the FM 2350 intersection on the east (right) side of the road; **Bull Creek Canyon** is best viewed with binoculars, in the bluffs of the Llano Estacado caprock, about 10 miles just north of west (left), at a distance of about 5 miles.

One of the Comanche hiding places along the caprock was **Bull Creek Canyon.** Typical of the kind of fastness that protected Indians camping in the face of the Llano Estacado, this is probably the place where the last band of Kwahadi Comanches under Quanah Parker hid in the winter of 1874 to 1875. U.S. soldiers discovered them here only with the help of three friendly Comanches—Wild Horse, Habbywake, and Toviah—who guided the army patrol from Fort Sill, Oklahoma, and persuaded Quanah to surrender and move to the reservation. The Comanche name for the canyon means "tule reed," or "bulrush"—a marsh plant, which suggests that dependable water was found along the creek at one time.

To reach **Courthouse Mountain** from **Bull Creek Canyon,** continue north on SH 669 to the SH 207 intersection at Post; take SH 207 north about 17.5 miles, or 3.5 miles past the Crosby County line; at this point, **Courthouse Mountain** will be the long, low hill that appears about 1 mile due west (left) and extends 0.5 miles northward, parallel to the road. Note also at this point that the high, red north wall of **Yellow House Canyon** will appear prominently to the north (ahead) about 3 miles on both sides of the highway. See chapter 6 for information on Yellow House Canyon.

Courthouse Mountain was a navigation marker for Indian travelers moving between Silver Falls and Mushaway. The old Comanche name for Courthouse Mountain seems to refer to a wind gap, probably noting the notch in the middle of the mountain. Notice that Courthouse Mountain is part of a longer formation, which is known locally as Indian Ridge.

To reach **Blanco Canyon** and **Silver Falls** from **Courthouse Mountain,** continue north on SH 207 about 16.5 miles to the U.S. 82/62 intersection at Ralls; take U.S. 82 east about 12.5 miles, through Crosbyton, to the intersection with FM 2591 on the north (left) side of the road; at this point, the road has descended about 200 feet into the **Blanco Canyon,** and you will see the white stratum for which the canyon is named. Proceed about 1 mile farther east on U.S. 62 to **Silver Falls Park,** which is on the south (right) side of the highway.

Blanco Canyon begins west of the Texas–New Mexico border as Agua Corriente, or "Running Water Draw." Below Plainview, Texas, the streambed is called **White River,** and the valley is Blanco Canyon. The English and Spanish names directly translate the Comanche place-name *Tosa Hunu?bi*, referring to the white caliche stratum that is visible in the canyon walls near their top edges.

The Kwahadi, or "Antelope," band of Comanches put up a strong defense in Blanco Canyon when pursued by the U.S. Army during 1871 to 1872. As the moon set around 1:00 A.M. on October 10, 1871, Indian raiders stampeded sixty-six horses from the cavalry herd, skirmishing effectively before disappearing onto the Llano. The next fall, the Kwahadis were surprised near the mouth of the canyon. Their camp was destroyed; many Indians and over three thousand of their horses and mules were captured. On the following night, warriors stampeded and recaptured their animals.

A traditional landmark in the canyon was **Silver Falls,** now within a fine roadside park that offers canyon views and short hikes. In Comanche, "white" and "silver" are signified by the same word, so it is possible that the falls as well as the river take their names from the Native tongue.

The falls were a favorite stopover on a route linking Indian hideouts in the Llano with the campsites in the Wichita Mountains of southwest Oklahoma. Quanah Parker's band camped here with the army patrol it surrendered to in spring 1875. Below the falls, the river winds down to the Salt Fork of the Brazos.

To reach **Quitaque Peaks** from **Blanco Canyon** and **Silver Falls,** return west to Crosbyton and Ralls on U.S. 62; take U.S. 62 north from Ralls about 22 miles to the SH 207 intersection at Floydada (to stay on these highways in town, follow Second Street north to Missouri Street east); take SH 207 north about 12 miles to the second SH 97 intersection, on the east (right) side of the road; take SH 97 east about

16 miles to the Caprock bluffs; at the bottom of the bluffs, **Quitaque Peaks** will appear to the southeast (right) at a distance of about 2 miles. Good views can be obtained by proceeding along SH 97.

One of the most famous Indian meeting places in the region was Quitaque. The spot takes its name from **Quitaque Peaks (Mounds),** distinctive five-hundred-foot hills that can be seen for miles and that marked the general route of north-south Indian travel along the flanks of the Llano Estacado. The Mounds are actually eroded outliers from the Llano formation. The curious name comes from the Comanche words *kwita ku?e,* "excrement summit." An early English translation is "Dung Hills," suggesting perhaps that the Indians were noting a resemblance to piles of horse or buffalo dung. According to the late Tom Wahnee, a Comanche medicine man, the name came about because Indian scouts had the habit of squatting while they were posted on top of the peaks. So much for the poeticism of Indian place-names!

In the well-watered valley north of the hills, Indians congregated to trade with Comancheros such as José Tafoya. They swapped hides, livestock, and human captives for flour, metal goods, ammunition, and whiskey carted from New Mexico. In reference to the sad plight of the many captives ransomed here, the Comancheros called the Quitaque canyonlands El Valle de las Lágrimas (Valley of Tears). The excellent quality of flint in the area also drew Indian toolmakers.

To reach the vicinity of **Tee Pee City** from **Quitaque Peaks,** continue east on SH 97 about 10.5 miles, through Flomot, to the SH 70 intersection; take SH 70 south about 16 miles to the U.S. 62 intersection at Matador; take U.S. 62 east about 10.5 miles, into the first major curve in the road; at this point, there is a bridge over Tee Pee Creek, and a roadside park.

Tee Pee City might sound like an Indian-themed tourist trap, but all the excitement here occurred over one hundred years ago. All that remains now is a few settlers' graves and a historical marker at the end of a private road, 6.7 miles northeast of the roadside park.

The place-name originated when settlers found tipi poles up and down along the creek, which had been a well-used campground of the Comanches.

As with several other prime Native campsites in northwest Texas, Indian occupation gave way to a buffalo hunter's station during the 1870s. Following the extermination of the bison, Tee Pee City evolved into a wild and wooly cowboy town, complete with saloon and dance hall girls. By around 1900, Tee Pee City had become such a den of iniquity that the management of the Matador Ranch, trying to keep its cowboys sober enough for work, bought the whole place and closed it down.

> To reach **Double Mountain** from **Tee Pee City,** return west on U.S. 62 to the U.S. 70 intersection at Matador; take U.S. 70 south about 89 miles, through Roaring Springs, Dickens, Spur, and Jayton, to the SH 610 intersection on the east (left) side of the road; take SH 610 east about 7.5 miles; this is the nearest approach to **Double Mountain,** which completely dominates the landscape to the northwest (left) 3 miles away.

Both peaks at **Double Mountain** rise about six hundred feet above the surrounding terrain. A closer look reveals that they were formed from one feature: The lowest point in the gap between them is considerably higher than the surrounding terrain. **Double Mountain** is the dominant landmark in the area for some twenty miles. The branch of the Brazos River that winds by about ten miles to the south is called the Double Mountain Fork, aptly named by American explorers approaching from the east. Possibly an Indian vision quest site, Double Mountain was proposed as the place for a conference between Southern Comanches and representatives from the Texas government in 1843.

Notable dates include 1849, when, while passing ten miles south of Double Mountain, U.S. Army Captain Randolph B. Marcy observed Indian signal fires communicating in several directions; and 1874, when Comanches returning from a raid to Mexico skirmished here with U.S. troops under Colonel Buell.

Kiowa Peak. Photo by Wayne J. Pate

To reach **Kiowa Peak** from **Double Mountain,** continue north-east on SH 610 about 12.5 miles to the U.S. 380 intersection at As-permont; take U.S. 380 east about 21 miles, through Old Glory, to the FM 617 intersection at the western edge of Rule; take FM 617 north about 11.5 miles, to the FM 2279 intersection on the west (left) side of the road. Note: Although FM 617 travels only north-south or east-west along section lines, it curves several times on the way to the FM 2279 intersection. Be alert to speed limits on tight curves, and watch the numbers of intersecting FM roads carefully to avoid getting lost. Take FM 2279 north about 5.5 miles to the FM 2229 intersection on the east (right) side of the road; at this point, **Kiowa Peak** is evident as a solitary peak to the west (left), 3.8 miles away.

Another area landmark is **Kiowa Peak,** which stands 462 feet over the Rolling Plains. The Indian association here is by name rather than specific events; it is one of only three natural features in the state bearing the Kiowa name. However, it is likely that the hill functioned as others did in the region for signaling, reconnaissance, and vision seeking.

> To reach **Medicine Mounds** from **Kiowa Peak,** take FM 2229 east about 8.8 miles the SH 6 intersection at O'Brien; take SH 6 north about 65 miles, through Knox City, Benjamin, and Crowell, to the U.S. 287 intersection at Quanah; take U.S. 287 east about 5.6 miles to the FM 1167 intersection on the south (right) side of the highway; take FM 1167 south about 7 miles to the third 90-degree curve; from this point, the **Medicine Mounds** site extends southward from Big Mound (lying just north of due west) to Cedar Mound, Third Mound, and Little Mound; all are less than 1 mile away.

Perhaps the most wonderous place on the Texas Rolling Plains, **Medicine Mounds** commands a long stretch of the Red River country. An excellent view of the mounds is had from the roadside park on U.S. 287 about six miles west of Chillicothe. Closer views are available by heading south from the highway on the grid of secondary roads, but keep to the public roads—the mounds are on private property.

The four mounds, from northwest to southeast, are named Big Mound, Cedar Mound, Third Mound, and Little Mound. Big Mound, the tallest, rises about 350 feet above the floor of Big Valley lying to the east. Four is the sacred number underlying Indian myth and ritual, and the presence of four hills here undoubtedly added to the significance of the location. The mounds marked a path of travel from the Wichita Mountain Indian encampments some seventy-five miles north in Oklahoma. In fact, the sacred Mount Scott at the eastern end of the Wichitas is clearly visible on most days from the top of Big Mound.

According to some of the old families that lived around the Medicine Mounds train depot, the relatively level area between Cedar and Third Mounds was a "racetrack" where Indian ran their horses; however, there is no independent corroboration of this belief. Nevertheless, Big Mound is generally considered the site of Comanche vision quests, dances, hunts, and medicine collecting, and the entire microenvironment is an excellent study in the natural features that attracted and sustained Indian populations.

A spring of gypsum water just north of the largest hill, dry since the 1930s, provided ready water, and two well-watered draws remain running south from the hills. This site contains wild onions, plums, mesquite, prickly pear, sumac, and snakeweed, as well as cottonwood, little bluestem grass, Indian breadroot, and the medicinal *pohóobi* (gray sage) and *ekapokowaapi* (red berry cedar, red cedar or juniper).

Apparently, an abundance of prairie dogs was once found in the area, giving rise to a Comanche place-name meaning "Prairie Dog Summit." This term was in turn extended as one of many Indian names for the nearby Red River, and it lives on in the title Prairie Dog Town Fork, used for the main course of the river upstream from this area.

Suggestions of Indian ritualism at the site include what looks like a toppled cairn (a heap of rocks) between Big and Cedar Mounds as well as a hole excavated in the bedrock at the top of Big Mound—although these features are not visible from any distance. Cairns were used by Plains Indians as markers and altars. Although its origin and function are uncertain, the hole may have been a place for vision questing, given its location near the southeast edge of the top of the mound.

From Medicine Mounds, a detour to visit the **Wichita Mountains National Wildlife Refuge** in Oklahoma will be worthwhile for enthusiasts of the Indian landscape. Named for the Wichita Indians whose villages were found here in the early 1800s, this beautiful pink granite range held significance for all the area tribes. One can see in approaching the Wichitas how mountain ranges on the Plains take on an islandlike or oasislike quality, holding forth the promise of cool air and cold water.

Locations to visit include two notable sites: first, Mount Scott on the eastern front of the range, which is the highest peak and a former place for Indian rituals; second, Bat Cave northeast of Indiahoma, which Comanches said was the lair of the mythological *Piamupits* (Giant Owl), the cannibal ogre who once imprisoned the

Medicine Bluffs. Photo by Daniel J. Gelo

buffalo. The ogre, however, is no longer troublesome. Free-ranging buffalo, as well as elk herds and a prairie dog colony, are viewable to car-bound visitors, evoking images of the Plains past.

When in the area, also see **Medicine Bluffs,** approachable by entering the Fort Sill military base at Key Gate, IH 44, exit 41 north of Lawton (ask the gatehouse guard for local directions). These spectacular cliffs were the site of vision quests and legends of the Kiowas and Comanches, and presumably other tribes. Wichita Indians once had a settlement of grass houses in the "Punchbowl" area north of the cliff edge.

To reach **Brushy Mound** and **Queens Peak** from **Medicine Mounds,** continue east and north on FM 1167 about 10 miles to the U.S. 287 intersection at Chillicothe; take U.S. 287 east about 108 miles, through Vernon, Electra, Iowa Park, Wichita Falls, Henrietta, and Bellevue, to a point exactly 4 miles east of the Montague County line; at this point, **Brushy Mound** is the prominent point directly northeast (left), about 0.3 miles from the highway.

To reach **Queens Peak** from **Brushy Mound,** continue east on U.S. 287 about 4.6 miles to the U.S. 81 intersection at Bowie; take U.S. 81 north about 4.6 miles; at this point, **Queens Peak** is clearly visible to the east (right) less than 1 mile away.

Brushy Mound and **Queens (Queen's) Peak** are two knolls in the Belknap Hills formation, each standing two hundred feet above their surroundings at a distance of 3.5 miles from each other. Together they command the route of passage between the Trinity and Red River drainages, and both are noted in local history as Indian lookouts. This area is also an excellent place to study the western Cross Timbers environment, which even today is thick in places with the dwarf oak growth that in former times was such an obstacle to east-west travel.

To reach **Spanish Fort** from **Queens Peak,** take U.S. 81 north about 3.7 miles, to the FM 1806 intersection just beyond Stoneburg; take FM 1806 east about 11.3 miles to the SH 175 intersection at Montague; take SH 175 north about 8.5 miles to the U.S. 82 intersection at Nocona; jog east (right) one block to the SH 103 intersection on the north (left) side of the highway; take SH 103 north and east about 16.8 miles through Hynds City, Rowland, and Valley View, to **Spanish Fort.**

One of the most interesting Indian village sites in all the Southwest is disguised by the name **Spanish Fort.** Anglos who settled the area after 1859 found Spanish artifacts at this location and assumed that the old ruins once visible here were the remains of a Spanish outpost. In fact, the old fort was built in the 1750s by the Taovayas, a subgroup of Wichita Indians. Indian fortifications of any size were probably very uncommon in the west, but here, on a flat clearing along the Red River, the Taovayas built wooden palisades, trenches, and a moat to defend their permanent village. They also set up a similar fortified village on the opposite (Oklahoma) side of the Red River.

In October 1757, the Indians turned away a four-hour attack by a Spanish force; they mocked the Spaniards from within their stronghold and even withstood fire from two cannons, which the Spaniards abandoned in their retreat. Disease and settlement pressure in the valley caused the Taovayas to abandon their fort by the 1840s; however, it was later rediscovered. During the early cattle drives, a wild town grew here, but it too was deserted. All traces of the old Indian fort are now gone from the ground surface, but the remaining Anglo ghost town hints at the mystery that the abandoned fort once conjured.

> To reach **Devil's Backbone** from **Spanish Fort,** return on SH 103 west and south to the U.S. 82 intersection at Nocona; take U.S. 82 east about 13.7 miles to the second SH 677 intersection on the left (north) side of the highway at Saint Jo; take SH 677 north and west about 1.5 miles, to the point where the road overlooks Katy Lake to the east (right); sight **Devil's Backbone,** the ridge starting north and east beyond the lake at a distance of 1 mile.

Not to be confused with the formations of the same name west of Austin or in southeast Kent County, the ridge called **Devil's Backbone** in Montague County was a lookout post for Kiowas and Comanches scouting the settlements and roads of the area from the 1850s until the mid-1870s.

> To reach **Jim Ned Lookout** from **Devil's Backbone,** return south on SH 677 about 3.2 miles, through Saint Jo to the FM 3206 intersection on the west (right) side of the road; take FM 3206 south about 7.5 miles, past the Dye community and the two prominent mounds that rise above it; the next mound, on the south side of the road, is **Jim Ned Lookout.**

Not much is known about the precise origin of the name **Jim Ned Lookout,** but it suggests that the knoll was an Indian reconnaissance place. Jim Ned was a Delaware Indian leader who served as a scout for the Texas militia during the 1840s. The name shows up farther west in the Texas landscape as well: There is a Jim Ned Creek east of Abilene, most likely also named for the Delaware scout.

> To reach **Comanche Peak** from **Jim Ned Lookout,** continue south on FM 3206 about 3 miles to the SH 455 intersection at Mallard; take SH 455 south about 7 miles to the FM 1655 intersection at Forestburg; take FM 1655 south about 16 miles to the IH 287 intersection at

Alvord; take IH 287 south about 11.5 miles to the SH 51 intersection at Decatur; take SH 51 south about 60 miles through Springtown, Weatherford, and Granbury; in Granbury, jog west 6 blocks on Pearl Street and turn south (left) on Morgan Street to access the SH 144 intersection; take SH 144 east (south) about 4 miles; from this point, **Comanche Peak** is the prominent rise to the southwest (right) less than 1 mile away.

Comanche Peak is useful in illustrating how, in the relatively level region of the Rolling Plains, certain less-than-dramatic heights could gain significance as landmarks. In 1846, after Texas joined the Union, the U.S. government sent its first delegation to attempt a treaty with the Comanches. This mesa was selected as the meeting place. Scouts had arranged the meeting, but the main party of delegates rode around and could not find the site for several days. Apparently, they were expecting a real mountain.

Elijah Hicks wrote in his journal, with frustration and relief, that the peak had "been found at last; but destitute of enchantment. Lo! It is a brushy hill!" Perhaps the Indians more easily read significance into this place, which included some caves in the limestone and a good view of the countryside.

To reach a view of **Boys Peak** from **Comanche Peak,** continue east (south) on SH 144 about 10 miles to the U.S. 67 intersection; take U.S. 67 west about 14.5 miles, through Glen Rose and Chalk Mountain, to the SH 220 intersection on the south (left) side of the road; take SH 220 south about 13.5 miles to the SH 6 intersection at Hico; take SH 6 west about 0.3 miles to the U.S. 281 intersection; take U.S. 281 south about 65 miles through Hamilton to the U.S. 183/190 intersection on the north (right) side of the road, north of Lampasas; take U.S. 183/190 north (west) about 6.5 miles; at this point, **Boys Peak** is the prominent hill to the northeast (right 90 degrees) about 3.5 miles away. Note: Do not confuse **Boys Peak** with Flat Top Peak in the foreground of this view, or with Twin Mountains, which may also be seen from this point but at 45 degrees right (due north), at a distance of 5 miles.

Boys Peak is the probable place where, in 1808, the early Anglo trader Anthony Glass found a natural cistern at the top of a hill. He was traveling with Comanches or Wichitas at the time and reported that the Indians believed the Great Spirit filled this water hole for their convenience.

A complete tour of the Rolling Plains ends with this view of **Boys Peak.** To finish the full circuit, continue on U.S. 190 west about 71 miles through San Saba to the U.S. 283 intersection at Brady; take U.S. 283 north about 45 miles to Santa Anna.

6

THE STAKED PLAINS

The Llano Estacado, or "Staked Plains," has long had a reputation as a forbidding and mysterious landscape. In earlier times, the phenomenally large stretches of truly flat, treeless short grass plains, with few obvious landmarks and limited water, presented a challenge to travelers. Access to the region was made difficult by an escarpment at the Llano's edges, with prominent cliff faces along sections of the eastern and western High Plains boundaries.

One theory behind the region's old Spanish name likened the escarpment face to the timber palisades of a fort. A more imaginative story roots the name in Coronado's expedition into the area in 1540—supposedly, the plains were so bare that the Spaniards had to carry along stakes and drive them in the ground every so often so that they could mark a trail home. It was many days across to the *ceja,* or "brow" (edge)—if you could find it, that is. Army captain Nicholas Nolan and his command of African American "buffalo soldiers" lost their way in August 1877; marching eighty-six hours without water, four died in the maddening dry heat, and the rest survived by drinking their horses' urine.

Nevertheless, Native American travelers knew several travel routes across the Llano. These pathways generally crossed the area from northwest in New Mexico to the southeast, following draws that in places were very faint and that elsewhere broke into open canyons—actually, into the headwaters of the great Texas rivers. Some would contain flowing water seasonally, but all would contain springs.

Several spring-fed lakes in the southern part of the area supplied travelers, as did seasonal rain-puddle ponds, or *playas*. By judging long-term rain cycles and the recent weather, Indian people could guess where water was likely to be found at any particular time and so choose the best path. They also knew to watch for signs that point to water, like the flight direction of doves at dusk.

Ancient traders crossed the Llano to link the Pueblos of New Mexico with easterly villages, such as those of the Caddoans in Kansas. Buffalo pelts, Osage orange wood (for bow making), flint arrowheads, and mineral paints are some of the items thought to have been traded. At the beginning of the historic period, the Puebloan people that the Spanish called Jumanos were still specialists in this trade.

Mounted Apaches and then Comanches invaded from the north after the mid-1600s. The horse Indians were perhaps more brazen in their travel, since the speed of riding had the effect of "shrinking" the distance between water holes; however, the Llano remained relatively dangerous and lightly populated. Although some corn may have been cultivated along the Canadian and Red Rivers between 1200 and 1500, Indian farming never took hold on the high, dry Llano.

How predictable game was in the area is hard to say. Reports have been made of fantastic herds of bison and antelope, yet, so have reports describing long stretches of scarcity. For the Indian traveler, game ambushed at the water holes was probably the best bet; animals could be taken on approach to a spring or pond before setting up camp there. Some locations thus became regular stopovers known to all the tribes.

Modern towns and roads reflect these ancient patterns, though not exactly. Lubbock is situated at one of the great crossroads of Indian trade. A few highways shadow the old routes closely, but most roads were built to serve the checkerboard of non-Indian settlements.

By the late 1800s, when county seats in much of the Llano were being established, the windmill pump gave settlers some freedom from water-hole locations. That same technology and the ranches and farms it spawned have lowered the water table so that the surface is drier than it was in old times. Water holes that remain may be salty or fouled with oil and farm runoff. Native grasses have given way to introduced varieties. The look of the high plains has changed dramatically since Indian days, but traces of the older Llano are still to be found along some of the back roads.

LAY OF THE LAND

The two most distinctive features of the Staked Plains region are its incredible flatness and the height of this "tabletop" surface above adjoining areas. The dramatic edge bluff is referred to in general as the Caprock Escarpment, or simply "the Caprock." However, that term is also applied specifically to the east face, whereas the southwest face is sometimes called the Mescalero Escarpment, and the northwest, the Canadian Escarpment.

About forty miles west of the Texas border in Lea County, New Mexico, the bluffs are thirty feet high, and their slope is gentle enough to climb by foot. Across the Llano and along the northeastern edge, the walls of Palo Duro and the neighboring canyons descend perpendicularly almost nine hundred feet to the Rolling Plains below.

Those approaching from below may be struck by the sheer verticalness, only to be impressed again by the sudden utter flatness "up on top" (the phrase used by local people living below). The level area extends continuously from just north of Amarillo to just south of Odessa; from east to west, it is framed roughly by Texas towns such as Quitaque and Gail, and by New Mexico towns such as Monument and Tucumcari. This area is about forty thousand square miles, nearly as large as the states of Maine and New Hampshire combined.

But the flatness is not absolute. Three types of features punctuate the surface up on top: sand hills, which occur with increasing frequency toward the southwest Llano, making the area around Kermit, Texas, and nearby Jal, New Mexico, seem like a desert; "draws," or natural drainage routes, generally running northwest to southeast (except in the Llano's northern quadrant, where they tend to run to the northeast), at intervals of eight to twenty-three miles; and lakes, over fifty thousand of which are scattered across the surface.

The sand hills have been greatly reduced in efforts to yield more productive farmland, but several areas have large stretches that are still untamed. Many are surprisingly rich in groundwater and wild game. Some of the largest trophy deer on record in Texas have been taken in the sand hills. While Euro-Americans came to view the sand hills as certain death traps, Indian people apparently never shared this view and camped in them frequently. These areas provided some of the last refuges for resistant Apaches and Comanches in the 1870s and 1880s.

Draws reveal the slight but definite slope of the entire Llano surface from northwest to southeast. These drainages, which range in depth from ten to sixty feet, were once rivers originating in the Sangre de Cristo Mountains of New Mexico. Massive late Pleistocene ice melts flowing south from the Colorado Rockies then carved the wide Pecos River Valley west of and far below the Llano surface. Flow of the more ancient rivers was diverted, leaving the draws we see today.

These low, sometimes subtle pathways are visible as one crosses them along modern highways; they were common travel routes for the Apaches, Comanches, and other aboriginal peoples. A number of the major draws held reliable water, such as Running Water Draw and Blackwater Draw in Bailey and Parmer Counties.

Of the fifty thousand lakes up on top, all but about one hundred are now playa lakes, or collections of rain and snow melt that swell and shrink with the seasons. Farmers have long had a love–hate relationship with these lakes, coveting the potential farmland they cover in wet times and giving thanks for the water they bear in times of drought. It is impossible to know exactly how many of the playas were originally spring fed and hence perennial in former days, but strong evidence suggests that depressions of no more than ten to fifteen feet frequently tapped into springwater when the water table was higher.

The existence of a hundred or so remaining spring-fed lakes on the Llano seems to be a well-kept secret, understandable given the value of groundwater in a region that suffered heavily during the "Dust Bowl" of the 1930s and the "Mini Dust Bowl" of the 1950s. A number of the smaller lakes still thrive on springwater, and as recently as the 1970s, the U.S. Geological Survey reported twenty-four spring-fed lakes in Parmer County alone.

Grasses of varying heights carpet the Llano. Short grasses such as grama and buffalo grass dominate, forming a dense sod in some areas, while medium grasses such as little bluestem are also visible in places where grazing has not reduced them. Stands of native grasses are best viewed at Rita Blanca and Kiowa National Grasslands northwest of Dalhart.

A startling variety of other plants is found among the grasses and especially around perennial water. Cactus and yucca species provided fruit, fiber, and soap for Indian inhabitants; edible tubers lie beneath the sod, and wildflowers add a riot of color. And despite the wide expanses of grassland, trees are numerous on the high plains along waterways: cottonwoods, hackberries, plums, oaks, pecans, willows, mesquites, and others. As a result of their seeds being swallowed and passed by ranging cattle, mesquites have taken over some former grasslands and now form extensive thickets. These thickets are not characteristic of the plains in Indian times.

Two final features of the Llano must be noted: the nearly constant wind and the immensity of the sky. With little surface resistance, the wind reaches speeds and causes sudden weather changes that are of legendary proportion. So steady and strong is the breeze that residents regard the day as "calm" when the wind speed drops below ten miles per hour. Regarding the quick downturns in temperature brought on by the arrival of cold air masses, or "northers," Llano natives like to say, "Sleep late, and miss two seasons!" The huge sky can be a source of intense beauty, providing magnificent sunsets that radiate brilliant colors all around the horizon for an hour or more.

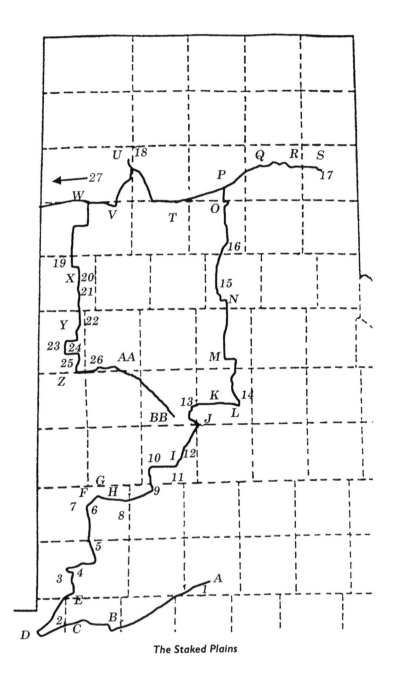

The Staked Plains

Sites

1. Big Spring
2. Blue Mt.
3. Whalen Lake
4. Shafter Lake
5. Monument Draw
6. Seminole Draw
7. Wardswell Draw
8. Cedar Lake
9. Frost, Saleh, and Gooch Lakes
10. Double Lakes
11. Guthrie Lake
12. Tahoka Lake
13. Yellowhouse Canyon sites
14. Blanco Canyon/Silver Falls
15. Tule Canyon
16. Palo Duro Canyon
17. Mobeetie
18. Old Tascosa
19. Tierra Blanca Draw
20. Frio Draw
21. Running Water Draw
22. Blackwater Draw
23. Coyote Lake
24. Baileyboro Lake
25. Muleshoe NWR
26. Bull Lake
27. Tucumcari

Cities and Towns

A. Big Spring
B. Odessa
C. Notrees
D. Kermit
E. Andrews
F. Seminole
G. Seagraves
H. Loop
I. Tahoka
J. Slaton
K. Ralls
L. Crosbyton
M. Floydada
N. Silverton
O. Claude
P. Panhandle
Q. Pampa
R. Laketon
S. Mobeetie
T. Amarillo
U. Boys Ranch
V. Vega
W. Adrian
X. Friona
Y. Muleshoe
Z. Needmore
AA. Littlefield
BB. Lubbock

While the Llano may strike newcomers as an expanse of endless emptiness, natives often see it as a place of immense freedom and limitless possibilities. Some think the terrain of the Llano might breed anarchical temperaments, mysticism, and an intense, personal attachment to the landscape not easily appreciated by outsiders.

EXPLORING THE LLANO

This tour starts in the city of **Big Spring** in southern Howard County, at the intersection of IH 20 and U.S. 87. The spring can be viewed in Comanche Trail City Park on the south edge of town, accessible from U.S. 87 and FM 700. Note: the spring is in the city park and not the adjacent Big Spring State Park.

Located where the Llano Estacado gives way to neighboring geographic zones, fabled **Big Spring** is the appropriate place to start our journey. With a huge volume of clear water, Big Spring was a natural crossroad of Indian trails. Comanche elders today recall that their ancestors approaching the springs from the north knew to look for the two hills rising on either side of the pool, now called Scenic and South Mountains—one of several "twin" features important in Indian navigation across Texas. The last Comanche raid on a Texas settlement was made nearby in 1879 by renegades from the Oklahoma reservation.

To reach **Blue Mountain** from the town of **Big Spring,** take IH 20 west about 60 miles to Odessa; continue on IH 20 about 3 miles past downtown Odessa and exit Loop 338 northbound; follow Loop 338 north about 3 miles to the intersection with SH 322; take SH 322 west about 21 miles to Notrees; continue west on SH 322 about 2 miles to the Winkler County line. At this point, the elevation of the highway will drop noticeably, about 80 feet—you have just descended from the Southwestern Caprock, at the natural boundary of the Llano Estacado. Continue west about 4 miles past the edge of the caprock descent for the best view of **Blue Mountain;** from this location, note its bluffs to the north (about 90 degrees to the right). For a better sense of the size and majesty of **Blue Mountain,** continue west on SH 322 about 15 miles to the SH 18 intersection at Kermit; take SH 18 north about 1 mile to the SH 115 intersection; take SH 115 north about 10 miles, to the road sign announcing Kermit Sandhills Park; by looking northeast of SH 115 (right at about a 40 degree angle), you can see the entire western face of **Blue Mountain** about 6 miles distant, extending in an arc for about 4 miles.

Blue Mountain is an especially high reach of the escarpment and a feature marking the southwest edge of the Llano. Scouts here had a good view of the Trans-Pecos country lying to the west. Within the mountain are two cave shelters containing pictographs from the historic period. The artwork, probably Comanche, includes handprints and some human figures. Springs that have gone dry once sustained campers here.

To reach **Whalen and Shafter Lakes** from **Blue Mountain,** continue on SH 115 north about 21 miles to the intersection with SH 181; take SH 181 north about 12.5 miles to the intersection with SH 176; take SH 176 west (road signs will indicate the distance to Eunice, New Mexico) about 1.5 miles; watch the south (left) side of the road for **Whalen Lake.** The shining lakebed will be fully visible for a very short distance in a slight depression, about 1 mile south of the highway. Proceed about 1.5 miles past the view of Whalen Lake to the intersection with FM 1967; take FM 1967 north (east) about 8 miles; the road will drop into a noticeable depression and then curve slightly to the north (left), to skirt the northern edge of **Shafter Lake.** Note: Several highways intersect at various places in the area between Kermit and Andrews. Check highway numbers carefully before changing roads; a few seconds spent double-checking is much less frustrating than having to backtrack.

Whalen and Shafter Lakes are typical of the south Llano lakes that offered good camping in a generally tough environment. Shafter Lake is named for Lieutenant Colonel William R. Shafter, who discovered it in fall 1875 while leading African American buffalo soldiers out of Fort Concho in a sweep of the Llano at the close of the Red River War. Shafter's expedition spelled the end of the southern Llano as an Indian sanctuary and the start of modern mapping of the region.

> To reach **Monument Draw** from **Shafter Lake,** continue on FM 1967 east about 4 miles beyond the lake to the intersection with SH 385; take SH 385 north about 2.8 miles, about 1 mile past the road sign indicating a turnoff to the community of Florey. **Monument Draw** is the minor depression clearly marked on a highway sign.

The southernmost of three important water sources that aided north-south travel in this area is **Monument Draw.** The draw is apparently so named because it runs westward to the vicinity of Monument Spring, near Monument, New Mexico.

> To reach **Seminole** and **Wardswell Draws** from **Monument Draw,** take SH 385 north about 12.5 miles. **Seminole Draw** is clearly marked by road signs. About 3 miles north of **Seminole Draw** on SH 385 is **Wardswell Draw,** which contains a historical marker in Hackberry Grove, a stand of trees in the draw where early settlers congregated to formally organize the town now called Seminole. It converges with **Seminole Draw** about 5 miles southeast of this point.

The middle of three arroyos (water-carved channels) aiding north-south travel, **Seminole Draw** contained about twenty large water holes, apparently scooped from the sand by Indians and referred to as Indian Wells or, later, Seminole Wells. The latter name was apparently the basis for the town name of Seminole. It probably refers to the Black Seminoles who served as scouts under Mackenzie, Bullis, and Shafter in the 1870s campaigns to sweep the Plains Indians out of the region (see **Las Moras Springs,** chapter 3, pp. 89–90). Shafter's unit received at least one formal commendation for its meritorious performance in the 1875 operation, and four Black Seminoles were awarded the Medal of Honor.

Nearby to the north were even more water holes, perhaps fifty, stretching for a mile and a half along **Wardswell Draw.** Livestock could be walked into the larger wells, and there was enough good water for several thousand head, no doubt a prime spot for Indians driving animals north from Mexico. Lieutenant C. R. Ward of the

Tenth Cavalry, a member of Shafter's 1875 expedition, is commemorated in the place-name. The springs in the area all went dry by 1925.

To reach **Cedar Lake** from **Wardswell Draw,** continue on SH 385 north about 19.5 miles through Seminole and to the SH 83 intersection at Seagraves; take SH 83 east about 17.5 miles, through the communities of Loop and Ashmore to the intersection with FM 1067; take FM 1067 south (right) about 5 miles. At the intersection of FM 1067 and FM 1066 is a granite historical marker for Cedar Lake. Here the lakebed will be in plain view to the south and southwest, but the best view of it is about 1 mile south, where the highway curves a second time, due east.

Cedar Lake is one of the best-known Staked Plains landmarks, and it is also the largest natural lake on the Llano Estacado. It was a headquarters for Indians and soldiers alike. Lieutenant John Bullis and a detachment of Black Seminole scouts surprised an Apache encampment here on October 17, 1875.

Some sources note this lake as the birthplace of Quanah Parker, son of a Comanche warrior and white captive mother, who resisted conquest to the very end of the Red River War before leading his people peacefully into the twentieth century. (Some historical studies citing interviews with Quanah have convincingly disputed this idea.) Excavations around the lakeshore by archaeologists from Texas Tech University have established that it was a major campground for the Comanches and their predecessors on the plains.

The place-name is a translation of Laguna Sabinas (Cedars Lake), so-called by the Comanchero traders out of New Mexico. Once, heavy vegetation attracted game here; early traveler John Cook likened the spot to a "tented circus." Springs feeding the lake were once sizeable streams, further dug out for watering. Aside from providing a prime camp, Cedar Lake stood at a convenient distance among other important water holes.

To reach **Frost Lake** from **Cedar Lake,** return north on FM 1067 to the intersection with SH 83; take SH 83 about 8 miles east, to the town of Welch, where the roadway becomes FM 2053; take FM 2053 east about 6.3 miles, to where this road turns north to converge with northbound FM 179; 1 mile north of this intersection the highway crosses the northwest end of **Frost Lake.**

One of the water holes leading east was **Frost Lake,** which worked with **Saleh Lake** and **Gooch Lake,** beyond sight to the north and northeast, like stepping stones toward the headwaters of the Double Mountain Forks of the Brazos River and the lower, more hospitable Rolling Plains.

To view the southwestern lake of **Double Lakes** from **Frost Lake,** take FM 179 north about 16 miles to the intersection with U.S. 82/380; take U.S. 82/380 east about 4 miles, to the intersection with FM 1328 on the north (left) side of the road; continuing east on U.S. 82/380 from this point, watch carefully for the southwestern **Double Lake** at a 45-degree angle to the left (northeast). A stop beside the road will be necessary for more than a quick glance of the lakebed.

Double Lakes is another "twin" feature notable in Texas navigation, although it is not always clear that Indian people perceived the same pairings of features that Anglo names note. The Double Lakes served as a link from both north to south and east to west. From the road, one of two lakes can be seen; its companion is beyond to the northeast. The Comancheros called this feature Lagunas Cuartas, or "Four Lakes," because the dry beds of **Twin Lakes** lie nearby, beyond sight about 1.5 miles south of the highway at the point where the southwestern Double Lake is visible.

To reach **Guthrie Lake** from **Double Lakes,** continue east on U.S. 82/380 about 10 miles to the U.S. 87 intersection at Tahoka; take U.S. 87 south about 2 miles. At the edge of town, the road will curve to the right (south-southwest) and remain straight for about a mile. This stretch of highway runs straight toward the northeast shore of the large, dry bed of **Guthrie Lake,** and the best view of the lake is found where the road curves due south (left) again.

Guthrie Lake and **Tahoka Lake** are further links in the Llano lake chain, lying together on a southwest to northeast line.

To reach **Tahoka Lake** from **Guthrie Lake,** return north on U.S. 87 and proceed about 4 miles, through Tahoka to the intersection with SH 400; take SH 400 north about 3 to 4 miles; slow down and watch carefully to the east-southeast (90 degrees to the right). The western bluffs of **Tahoka Lake** and brief glimpses of its shallow waters will come into view; more than a glance will require a roadside stop.

Another place to view **Tahoka Lake** is about 4 miles farther north on SH 400, just short of a slight curve to the right. A short draw opens here to provide a brief glimpse of the northern half of the lake, at a distance of about 2 miles.

To reach **Yellow House Canyon** from **Tahoka Lake,** continue on SH 400 north about 11.5 miles, through the town of Wilson to the intersection with U.S. 84 at Slaton; take U.S. 84 west (northwest) about 7.7 miles to the intersection with FM 835 on the north (right side) of the road; take FM 835 north about 2.5 miles to encounter **Yellow House Canyon** at the west end of Buffalo Springs Lake.

Yellow House Canyon is best understood as a linear complex of sheltered water-hole sites aiding travel across the Llano. The English name is derived from the equivalent Casas Amarillas, a reference to some remarkable rock formations along the north side of the draw about sixty-five miles northwest of Lubbock. Yellow House was also known to the Comancheros as Cañon del Rescate, "Ransom Canyon," for here the Comanches brought captives to trade for merchandise. The Comanches' own place-name was more innocent sounding, meaning "trader's creek."

To bypass additional **Yellow House Canyon** sites in Lubbock, continue on FM 835 about 1.5 miles to the FM 835/FM 1729 intersection; proceed north on FM 1729 about 6.8 miles to the intersection with U.S. 62/82/114.

To view more locations along **Yellow House Canyon (Punta de Agua** and **Lubbock Lake),** continue on FM 835, which turns west and is called Buffalo Road beyond Yellow House Canyon at the FM 835/FM 1729 intersection; take FM 835 for about 7.5 miles to the U.S. 87 (Avenue A) intersection in Lubbock; take U.S. 87 (Avenue A) north about 3.2 miles; continue beyond the U.S. 82 intersection (Parkway

Drive); once past the intersection, keep to the access road all the way to the entrance to Mackenzie State Park.

Running roughly parallel to Yellow House Canyon to the north is another key passageway, Agua Negra, now called **Blackwater Draw;** this draw turns south to join Yellow House at the northeast corner of Lubbock. The junction, known as **Punta de Agua,** "Point of Water," was a popular Indian and Comanchero rendezvous and a bivouac point for the U.S. Cavalry.

This spot lies within Lubbock's Mackenzie Park, accessible from East Broadway and Avenue A. The actual junction is on the Meadowbrook Municipal Golf Course, but one can approach the water below the golf course by taking the park road south past Joyland Amusement Park and under U.S. 82 to a large impoundment. Downstream of the junction, the stream becomes the Double Mountain Fork of the Brazos.

To reach **Lubbock Lake** from **Punta de Agua,** exit Mackenzie Park at the south end of the park road where it intersects with East Broadway; take East Broadway west about 0.5 miles to the intersection with U.S. 87 (Avenue A); take U.S. 87 (Avenue A) north about 0.5 miles to the intersection with 4th Street on the west (left) side of the road; take 4th Street about 1 mile west to the intersection with U.S. 84 (Avenue Q); take U.S. 84 (which bears left to become Clovis Road) north about 2.7 miles to the intersection with Indiana Avenue; exit onto the access road running west from the U.S. 84/Indian Avenue intersection and underneath Loop 289; proceed west and north about 0.5 miles to **Lubbock Lake Landmark State Historical Park.**

Also of interest is **Lubbock Lake** (no longer an actual body of water) on the northwest edge of Lubbock. Near this site was the definitive battle in the brief Comanche uprising of 1877 called the Hunter's War. On March 18, renegades from the Fort Sill reservation under Black Horse were caught at their campsites near Lubbock Lake after attacking several buffalo-hunting parties and killing one hunter. They were subjected to an all-day fight by stalking frontiersman.

At Lubbock Lake Landmark State Historical Park, layers of the earth reveal artifacts and bones left by early hunters. Photo by Daniel J. Gelo

The site is perhaps more famous for Paleo-Indian occupation dating back twelve thousand years, evident from numerous Clovis, Folsom, and Plainview points discovered here. Fossils and artifacts are exhibited in the Robert A. Nash Interpretive Center. The park is open Tuesday–Saturday, 9–5; Sunday, 1–5. For admission and information, call (806) 765-0737. Archaeological excavations here are sometimes open to guided tours; call ahead for information.

To rejoin the main route to **Blanco Canyon,** return toward the U.S. 84/Indiana Avenue intersection but follow signs for Loop 289; take Loop 289 north, east, and southeast about 6.3 miles to the U.S. 62/82/114 intersection; take U.S. 62/82/114 east (northeast) about 11 miles to the intersection with FM 1729.

To reach **Blanco Canyon** and **Silver Falls** from the **Yellow House Canyon sites,** take U.S. 62/82/114 east from the FM 1729 intersection about 32.5 miles, through the towns of Lorenzo, Ralls, and Crosbyton,

Silver Falls. Photo by Wayne J. Pate

to the intersection with FM 2591 on the north (left) side of the road. At this point, the road has descended about 200 feet into the **Blanco Canyon,** and you will see the white stratum for which the canyon is named. Proceed about 1 mile farther east on U.S. 62 to **Silver Falls Park,** on the south (right) side of the highway.

Lying parallel and to the north of Yellow House is a similar draw-canyon complex, **Blanco Canyon.** This landform begins west of the Texas–New Mexico border as Agua Corriente, or "Running Water Draw." Below Plainview, Texas, the streambed is called **White River,** and the valley is Blanco Canyon. The English and Spanish names directly translate the Comanche place-name *Tosa Hunuʔbi̱,* referring to the white caliche stratum that is visible in the canyon walls near their top edges.

The Kwahadi, or "Antelope," band of Comanches put up a strong defense in Blanco Canyon when pursued by the U.S. Army during 1871 to 1872. As the moon set around 1:00 A.M. on October 10, 1871, Indians stampeded sixty-six horses from the cavalry herd, skirmishing effectively before disappearing onto the Llano. The next fall, the

Kwahadis were surprised near the mouth of the canyon—their camp was destroyed. Many Indians and over three thousand of their horses and mules were captured. On the following night, warriors stampeded and recaptured their animals.

A traditional landmark in the canyon was **Silver Falls,** now within a fine roadside park that offers canyon views and short hikes. In Comanche, "white" and "silver" are signified by the same word, so it is possible that the falls as well as the river take their names from the Native tongue. The falls were a favorite stopover on a route linking Indian hideouts in the Llano with the campsites in the Wichita Mountains of southwest Oklahoma. In spring 1875, Quanah Parker's band camped here with the army patrol it surrendered to. Below the falls, the river winds down to the Salt Fork of the Brazos.

To reach **Tule Canyon** from **Blanco Canyon,** with more excellent views of **Blanco Canyon,** return west on U.S. 62/82/114 to the SH 651 intersection at Crosbyton; take SH 651 north about 10 miles to the intersection with SH 193—this junction occurs in the bottom of a broad stretch of Blanco Canyon; take SH 193 west about 8.5 miles to the SH 207 intersection at the Cone community; take SH 207 north about 49 miles through Floydada to the intersection with SH 86 at Silverton— the crossing of Blanco Canyon is evident about 6.5 miles north of Cone; take SH 86 west about 4 miles to the intersection with SH 207; take SH 207 north about 6 miles to **Tule Canyon** below Mackenzie Reservoir. The sudden drop from the Llano and the finlike red rock formations here are spectacular.

The next east-west passageway across the Staked Plains, along the Prairie Dog Town Fork of Red River, is the most dramatic and rugged. The Comanche name that gave rise to the English one, "(Prairie Dog) Mound Summit River," referred to the Medicine Mounds sacred site lying farther downstream (see chapter 5, pp. 140–41). The first part of this system encountered is **Tule Canyon,** a long side canyon adjoining Palo Duro Canyon from the south. With its sweet water and freestanding columns of red sandstone, the enchanting chasm was a refuge for Wichita, Comanche, and Cheyenne travelers seeking escape from cold north winds on the Llano. At or somewhat east of the place where SH 207 now

Caliche Bluffs, Blanco Canyon. Photo by Wayne J. Pate

Palo Duro. Photo by Wayne J. Pate

crosses, an Indian trail across the canyon narrows was conspicuous when explorer Peter Custis rode through in 1806.

To reach **Palo Duro Canyon** from **Tule Canyon,** continue north on SH 207 about 17 miles. From the Llano edge on the south, the roadway drops 900 feet into a canyon complex extending about 9 roadway miles to the north rim.

Palo Duro Canyon runs along the Red River. With its wide panoramas, red walls, and curious rock formations, this is one of the most spectacular features in the entire Southwest. Two of the most famous incidents of the Red River War occurred here. In August 1874, Cheyennes charged a large pursuing force under General Nelson Miles before taking positions along the crests of the canyon. Though outgunned, the warriors bought time for their families to abandon camp in Tule Canyon and scramble up the canyon walls to safety on the open Llano. The following month, troops under Colonel Ranald Mackenzie sneaked upon a large camp of Kwahadi Comanches who were settling into the deep, protective rift for the winter. Though few Indians were killed or captured, their horse herd was driven to Tule Canyon and destroyed, leaving the Kwahadis crushed once and for all. The last Comanche holdouts surrendered by the following spring.

Around the Red River and on the Canadian to the north, archaeology reveals several settlements of round and rectangular houses known collectively as the Antelope Creek Focus. These prehistoric Indian cultures were previously thought to have been corn farmers who migrated into the area from the Caddoan east or Puebloan west during a wet spell, circa 1200. Now it is thought that the period was dry and that the people practiced not heavy farming but various mixtures of adaptation, including buffalo hunting, seed gathering, corn gardening, and trading. The Antelope Creek people disappear from the prehistoric record suddenly, around 1500.

To reach **Mobeetie** from **Palo Duro Canyon,** take SH 207 north from Palo Duro Canyon about 32 miles through the towns of Claude and Conway to the intersection with U.S. 60 at Panhandle; take U.S. 60 east (northeast) about 34 miles to the intersection with SH 152 on the east (right) side of the road, just beyond Pampa; take SH 152 east about 23.5 miles through the communities of Heaton and Laketon to the intersection with FM 48 on the north (left) side of the road in **Mobeetie.** The original town site is directly south of this point; New

Mobeetie is about 1.3 miles north on FM 48. To view Sweetwater Creek, continue east (south) on SH 152 about 2.6 miles to the creek crossing.

For anyone traveling east and off the Caprock, an important stop between the Red and Canadian River drainages was the Sweetwater Branch of the North Fork, Red River (Sweetwater Creek) around **Mobeetie.** Contrary to several historical sources, the name *Mobeetie* does not mean "sweet water" in an Indian language. The name comes from *mubitai*, which literally means "nose hole" in Comanche, but is their way of saying "walnut," since a split walnut resembles nostrils. This "Walnut River" was a beloved sanctuary for the Indians, and it is a place where the Sun Dance was repeatedly held.

Kiowas, who called the river Maggot Creek, staged dances along the stream in 1869, 1873, and 1876. Comanches generally did not conduct sun dances during the contact period but sometimes joined the Kiowas in the Walnut River rituals.

Cheyennes also camped on this creek, as Lieutenant Colonel George Armstrong Custer discovered in spring 1869 while attempting to force them onto the reservation in Indian Territory (western Oklahoma). Such a favored location attracted buffalo hunters in the early 1870s, and their store and camp of skin tents became known as Hide Town, giving rise to the wild frontier town of Mobeetie and the Fort Elliott army post. The old settlement was badly damaged by a tornado in 1898, and in 1929, much of the town shifted north two miles (New Mobeetie) so as to lie on the newly built railroad.

To reach **Old Tascosa** from **Mobeetie,** return to the SH 60 intersection east of Pampa; take SH 60 west (southwest) about 66 miles through Panhandle and downtown Amarillo (where the highway becomes Amarillo Boulevard) to the intersection with FM 1061 on the northwest side of Amarillo; take FM 1061 north about 35 miles through the scenic Canadian River Breaks to the intersection with SH 385; take SH 385 north across the Canadian River about 1.7 miles to road signs to Boys Ranch and **Old Tascosa** on the east (right) side of the road; turn right, and the site of **Old Tascosa** is less than 0.5 miles ahead.

Old Tascosa was a legendary meeting spot for Indians and Comanchero traders on an easy ford of the Canadian River formerly
known as Bold Crossing. Live springs along Atascosa (or Tascosa)
Creek furnished fresh water to tide over travelers. The creek's name
is Spanish for "boggy creek," so called because of the quicksand
where it joined the river. Traders knew that if they built a fire when
they arrived at the site, by morning they would be surrounded by
Indians eager to trade buffalo hides and perhaps white captives for
beads, cloth, and metal goods.

Once the Comanches surrendered for reservation life, non-
Indian settlement was pioneered mainly by Hispanic shepherds
from New Mexico. Their 1876 "plaza" evolved into a wild 1880s
frontier town complete with cowboy gunfights and a cemetery called
Boot Hill. A virtual ghost town by the 1930s, Old Tascosa was revived as Cal Farley's Boys Ranch, a renowned home and school
for underprivileged youths. Local history is exhibited in the Julian
Bivins Museum at Boys Ranch, open daily year-round.

In concluding the **Staked Plains** tour, two optional extensions from
Old Tascosa are presented. Continue with the following directions to
view the series of draws and water holes used by Indians traversing the
far west reaches of the Llano Estacado. To visit **Tucumcari Mountain**
in New Mexico, proceed to page 171.

To reach **Tierra Blanca Draw** from **Old Tascosa**, take SH 385 south
about 24.5 miles; stay on SH 385 past the FM 1061 intersection to
the town of Vega; take IH 40 west about 13.3 miles to the SH 214
intersection at Adrian on the south (left) side of the highway; take
SH 214 south about 44 miles; at this point, SH 214 will cross **Tierra
Blanca Draw**. To reach **Frio Draw** from **Tierra Blanca Draw**, continue south on SH 214 about 14 miles, to the town of Friona; continue
south through town to its southern edge, where SH 214 crosses **Frio
Draw**.

Tierra Blanca Draw and its **Frio Draw** branch are the westward extensions of the Prairie Dog Town Fork of Red River running
through Palo Duro Canyon and beyond. As such, the two draws here

were probable routes for Indian people making their way between Palo Duro and Tucumcari or among the springs of the Portales Valley in New Mexico, where Portales Spring and Tiban Spring marked the way to the famous Indian campsite on the Pecos River called Bosque Redondo, near Fort Sumner.

To reach **Running Water Draw** from **Frio Draw,** continue south on SH 214 about 10.3 miles; at this point, SH 214 crosses **Running Water Draw.** To reach **Blackwater Draw** from **Running Water Draw,** continue south on SH 214 about 18.2 miles through Muleshoe to a point about 1 mile south of the town center; where SH 214 curves left from southwest back to due south is a wide swath of sand hills, which are the remains of **Blackwater Draw.**

Running Water Draw and **Blackwater Draw,** headstreams of the Blanco Canyon–White River and the Yellow House Canyon–Brazos River, respectively, were avenues for travel from Central Texas up into the Portales Valley in New Mexico.

To reach **Coyote Lake** from **Blackwater Draw,** continue south on SH 214 about 5.7 miles to the FM 746 intersection; take FM 746 west about 10 miles to the FM 1731 intersection; take FM 1731 south about 2.5 miles; at this point, the west end of **Coyote Lake** will appear due east (left) of the road.

Coyote Lake is one of the largest natural lakes on the Llano. Though the water is saline, this was a favorite camping place of the Comanches; however, it was later taken over by buffalo hunters and then the XIT Ranch, which was established in the early 1880s when the state of Texas appropriated and sold off the land to raise funds for the state capitol building.

To reach **Baileyboro Lake** from **Coyote Lake,** continue south on FM 1731 about 7 miles, to the FM 298 intersection; take FM 298 east about 5.8 miles, to the FM 2487 intersection; take FM 2487 south about 1.3 miles; at this point **Baileyboro Lake** will be visible on the east (left) side of the road in a slight depression about 300 yards away.

Coyote Lake. Photo by Wayne J. Pate

To reach **Muleshoe National Wildlife Refuge** from **Baileyboro Lake**, return to the intersection of FM 2487 and FM 298; take FM 298 east about 5.5 miles to the SH 214 intersection at Needmore; take SH 214 south about 5.8 miles to the entrance to

Muleshoe National Wildlife Refuge, marked on both sides of the highway.

To reach **Bull Lake** from **Muleshoe National Wildlife Refuge,** continue south on SH 214 about 2.5 miles to the FM 37/54 intersection; take FM 37/54 east about 14.2 miles; pass the FM 303 intersections running south (right) and north (left) from FM 54; at this point, FM 54 curves south and then east. **Bull Lake** will come into view on the north (left) side of the highway and will remain in sight for about 1 mile.

Additional waters assumed to have sheltered Indian campers making their way across the Staked Plains include **Baileyboro Lake,** the three saline lakes within **Muleshoe Refuge** (from north to south: Pauls, Goose, and White), and **Bull Lake.**

To return to **Lubbock** and other points south and east, continue east on FM 54 about 5.8 miles to the U.S. 84 intersection west of Littlefield; take U.S. 84 east (southeast) about 35.7 miles to Lubbock. This concludes the Staked Plains draws and water holes optional route.

To reach **Tucumcari Mountain** from **Old Tascosa,** take SH 385 south about 24.5 miles through downtown Vega to the intersection with IH 40; take IH 40 west about 77 miles to Tucumcari, New Mexico; **Tucumcari Mountain** is the most conspicuous peak alongside IH 40 about 1 mile south of town.

By driving west from Tascosa, travelers retrace the route of countless Indian and Comanchero adventurers off the Staked Plains and into northern New Mexico. A key feature on this route is **Tucumcari Mountain** at Tucumcari. A few different Apache and Comanche derivations for the name have been proposed, but according to the most reliable information from Comanche elders, the original name was *tukamukatu*, "ambush."

The military explorer Captain Randolph B. Marcy noted the site while leading settlers toward California in 1849. Marcy reported that two peaks were actually called Tucumcari by the Indians. The second of these might have been little Bulldog Mesa immediately south or the much more dramatic Mesa Redonda, visible some

seven miles farther south. In any case, the high spots allowed
Indians command of the broad valley passageway, with permanent
water found nearby at Tucumcari Lake. This site marked the way to
the wilderness of the Rocky Mountains and the riches of Taos and
Santa Fe.

7

MOUNTAINS AND BASINS

I n Texas west of the Pecos River, one encounters a landscape that, aside from perhaps the High Plains, best matches the cinematic image of the American West. This area is essentially a southeastern extension of the great basin and range country that runs from the western edges of the Great Plains to the coastal mountains of the Pacific. In geographic and cultural terms, the region has much more in common with New Mexico or Utah than it does with the eastern part of the Lone Star State.

The trenchlike Pecos forms a traditional eastern boundary of this rugged area. When approaching the river from the east along modern roads, it is often possible to sense the drop from the Edwards Plateau. In fact, the basin character of the landscape extends well east of the Pecos River in some places. Beyond the river to the west are vast stretches of level desert punctuated with mesas and dry, rocky mountain clusters. The state boundary on the north of the region is totally artificial; on the south and west, the Rio Grande forms an edge that is also arbitrary, since the same geography extends beyond it in Mexico. The Rio Grande is really a pathway of often more hospitable land through the desert, rather than a boundary between different physical zones.

The activity of prehistoric Indian peoples was strongly dictated by the presence of the rivers. Between six thousand and one thousand years ago, the homes of Archaic foragers were the wide shallow caves found where the Pecos and Devil's Rivers join the Rio Grande. These Lower Pecos people were skilled desert dwellers who lived on rabbits and other small game, as well as a wide variety of desert plants. (For our purposes, the Lower Pecos area is best approached from the southeast and is therefore covered in chapter 3— see **Seminole Canyon,** pp. 90–91).

Later, other cultures occupied the Rio Grande corridor, cultures that probably had much in common with the ancestors of the Pueblo Indians of the modern Southwest. Around one thousand years ago, the Jornado Mogollon people extended their range into West Texas from a core area in present southern New Mexico. The Mogollon were corn gardeners and hunters living in pit houses and rectangular adobe apartment dwellings. They prospered in Texas for a long stretch when climatic conditions were favorable. At times, they were able to settle well away from the Rio Grande, in the Hueco Bolson east of El Paso, selecting low spots where the soil below surface remained damp after desert showers washed through.

According to early Spanish accounts, another group with probable Pueblo origins was the Jumanos, who maintained farming villages at the juncture of the Rio Grande and Rio Conchos near Big Bend. Other members of this culture lived as mobile hunters and traders, ranging across much of Texas and linking other tribal populations with their commerce.

The Tigua Indians who presently live in the El Paso suburb of Ysleta are descendants of another wave of Puebloan settlers, refugees who arrived in present Texas in 1680 from an Indian revolt farther up the Rio Grande. The Tiguas left their rock paintings among those of earlier settlers; they hunted widely across the basin and ranges; and they grew corn in the desert like the Mogollon did. In 1990, author Dan Gelo was shown a place way out in the desert that had been used for corn gardening by some Tiguas well into the twentieth century; it was even fenced!

By the 1650s, Apaches had moved into the Mountains and Basin region, and also into much of western and Central Texas from the north, seizing if not disrupting the Jumano trade network and eventually absorbing some of the Jumano population. Within a century,

Comanches were following the Apaches into the region, driving many of them south and west into the mountains; the Kiowas then followed the Comanches. Neither of the latter two groups called the Mountains and Basins home, but both frequently traveled through or raided in the region.

All of the historic "newcomers" continued to encounter Puebloan peoples along the Rio Grande. The story of Indian life in the Mountains and Basins was therefore a turbulent one during the historic period, made only more tumultuous with the advance of Hispanic and Anglo settlers.

Of all the regions of Texas, the Mountains and Basin area preserves the clearest sense of what the world looked like in Indian days. The huge scale of the country minimizes modern objects such as roadways, power lines, and barns. It is not too hard to imagine Tiguas dragging slain deer through the arroyos and Apaches scouting from the Davis Mountain peaks.

LAY OF THE LAND

In gauging the feel of the land here, it is worthwhile to start with consideration of the region's names. The modern temptation to talk about the "Trans-Pecos" suggests wrongly that Indian people may have recognized the river as a boundary. It certainly was an obstacle for them. In earlier times, it was so deep and swift that they crossed judiciously at only certain spots, such as at Horsehead Crossing. The Pecos, however, also favored north-south travel. In this case, the Indian perception was probably one of moving through the region rather than along its edge, for several key features such as Castle Gap, Willow Springs, and Johnson Draw lie east of the river.

Our preferred term, "Mountains and Basins," describes an alternating pattern evident from topographic maps, though this image does not always seem appropriate from the ground. From some places on the surface, the region appears simply as a vast desert expanse with mountains far on the edge.

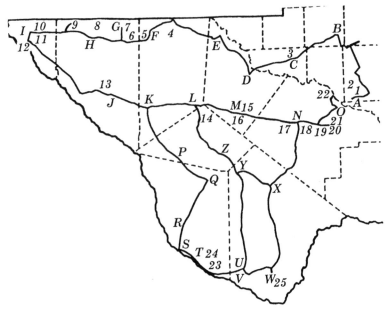

Mountains and Basins

Sites

1. King Mt.
2. Castle Mt.
3. Willow Springs
4. Ojo de San Martin
5. Guadalupe Peak, Capitan Bluff
6. Salt Basin
7. Las Cornudas Mts.
8. Ojo de Cuervo
9. Hueco Tanks
10. Sand Hills
11. La Loma de Barro
12. Tigua Reservation
13. Small Station
14. Gomez Peak
15. Toyah Creek
16. San Solomon Springs
17. Lake Leon
18. Comanche Springs
19. Tunas (Tunis) Springs
20. Darrel's Peak
21. Squawteat Peak
22. Horsehead Crossing
23. River Road
24. Big Bend Ranch State Park
25. Big Bend National Park

Cities and Towns

A. McCamey
B. Odessa
C. Monahans
D. Pecos
E. Orla
F. Pine Springs
G. Dell City
H. Cornudas
I. El Paso
J. Sierra Blanca
K. Van Horn
L. Kent
M. Balmorhea
N. Fort Stockton
O. Girvin
P. Valentine
Q. Marfa
R. Shafter
S. Presidio
T. Redford
U. Terlingua
V. Study Butte
W. The Basin
X. Marathon
Y. Alpine
Z. Fort Davis

The visual effect is deceptive, as the massiveness of the mountains and their distance become difficult to judge. In old accounts, travelers consistently estimate the distance of mountains in the region as perhaps a day's ride, only to reach them two or more days later. Although travel time is now compressed with the automobile, a car's speed does not necessarily minimize the deceptive quality of the landscape. The pavement may roll away beneath one's vehicle for several hours in reaching a landmark that looks to be but an hour away. Mountain ranges may even seem to retreat as they are approached.

The clarity of the desert air, unusual to people from outside the region, contributes to this odd sensation. Mountains on the horizon in this region lend a sense of immensity and grandeur that is absent on the Great Plains. They stand tall in one's field of vision despite the curvature of the earth, whereas on the Plains that curvature normally limits sight to about six miles, where nothing stands beyond.

The land is also marked by ruggedness and contrasts, sometimes stark and sometimes mild. A friend of author Wayne Pate who is an avid hiker describes the area as "all the cactus and jagged limestone you can eat." Huge salt flats, the remnants of prehistoric seas, extend south and west from the Guadalupe Mountains, their stark white surfaces shimmering in even partial sunlight. The gray Guadalupe range, an immense Permian reef rising three thousand feet above the surrounding landscape, is approached over fifty miles of desert and low hills.

Desert flora extends right to the visitor's center at the mouth of McKittrock Canyon, but less than two miles farther along, a different world is found, featuring a live creek, cooler air, towering evergreens, and more abundant wildlife. Two living rivers, the Delaware and Black, emerge to run east-northeast toward the Pecos. Similar natural surprises are among the other mountain chains, of which there are several: the Franklins, Huecos, Delawares, Apaches, Quitman, and Finlays, all the way into Big Bend, the Davis, Glass, Santiago, Chalk, Christmas, Chinati, Sierra Vieja, and Chisos ranges.

The many basin areas lying between the mountain chains, and the settlements they contain, can be quite distinctive. For instance, the towns of Alpine, Marfa, and Fort Davis, all in the Big Bend area, each has its own personality. No one would confuse Presidio with Lajitas, though both lie by the Rio Grande, and the tiny hamlets of Orla and Mentone, both within sight of Guadalupe Peak, are unmistakable.

Some generalizations are still possible. Throughout most of the lower elevations of the region, a Chihuahuan desert ecology prevails. Rainfall rates are low, ranging from sixteen inches annually on the eastern edge of the region to eight inches or less around El Paso. These figures include the snows that sometimes dust the mountains in midwinter. In general, conditions are dry; in fact, Wink in Winkler County, in the northeast corner of the area, holds the distinction of seeing the driest weather on record in Texas: only 1.76 inches of rainfall for all of 1956. What little moisture there is falls on rocks and soils of varied origin.

In the basins, the earth consists of windblown deposits of relatively young (Quarternary) age. The mountains are composed of a confusion of Precambrian outcrops and igneous formations from many periods. The scant rainfall and harsh soils support hardy bunch grasses—grama, burro, tussock, and salt grass—interspersed with cactus and many shrub species, including mesquite, yucca, creosote bush, acacia, agave, sotol, catclaw, and cenizo. Almost everywhere, wildflowers come alive after the rain showers. In the mountains, the dryland grasses and shrubs cover the lower slopes, but trees such as juniper, oak, piñon pine, and ponderosa pine may dominate the highest reaches.

Perhaps the region's most notable feature is its low population. Outside of the highly urbanized El Paso–Juarez corridor, the Mountains and Basins area contains the emptiest acreage in the state. All of Loving County is home to only one hundred people. Five or six cars on the stretch of highway between El Capitan and Van Horn would be tantamount to a traffic jam. Therefore, it is more important here than in the other Texas regions to check the roadworthiness of vehicles before traveling. A breakdown in some places could mean a roadside wait of many hours and a repair layover of even longer.

Yet, no part of Texas is more worth the time and effort of exploration. Whether the immediate terrain is flat desert or high mesa, the driver is hard-pressed to avoid wondering what lies farther along. Here is a landscape that is overwhelming in its ability to remain mysterious and to draw the imaginative traveler back again and again.

EXPLORING THE TRANS-PECOS

This tour begins near Rankin, McCamey, and Crane, south and southeast of Midland-Odessa, with a view of **King and Castle Mountains.** **King Mountain** can be seen well from at least four vantage points: (1) from the town of McCamey, where **King Mountain** is the massive mesa that rises just slightly east of due north at a distance of about 4.5 miles; (2) a roadside picnic area on SH 385, about 9 miles northwest of McCamey, by looking just north of due east; (3) from FM 2463, about 5 miles north of the intersection with SH 67, on the west (left) side of the road; (4) from the intersection of SH 329 with FM 2463, by looking southwest.

To begin the recommended route for the **Mountains and Basins Region,** the best point from which to view **King Mountain** is via the fourth vantage point. To see **Castle Mountain** from the same location, simply shift your view almost due west toward the other large mesa lying northwest of King Mountain. The distinctive feature of **Castle Gap** separates the mountains.

The pass through **Castle Mountain** is the famous **Castle Gap,** the landmark through which the Comanches traveled on their way to Horsehead Crossing on the Pecos River (about twelve miles westsouthwest) on their perennial raids into northern Mexico. This route has long been known as the Western Comanche Trace. In the nineteenth and early twentieth centuries, physical evidence remained of Comanche travel in the form of ruts made by the Indians' dragging their travois year after year along the same route.

Although no such marks are found today, it is easy to envision hundreds of Comanche warriors and their families moving across the dry and seemingly infinite flats, then catching sight of this landmark, a sure sign that there was water ahead. The Comanche name for the pass means "water gap," suggesting either that it pointed to the river or that fresh water could be found within.

To reach a view of possible evidence of the **Western Comanche Trace** from **Castle Mountain,** proceed on SH 329 north from the SH 329/FM 2463 intersection about 7.8 miles to the intersection with FM 1492; take FM 1492 north about 18 miles, to the intersection with FM 1787; take FM 1787 east about 4 miles, to the intersection with FM 1788.

At the FM 1787 and FM 1788 intersection, you will notice that the surrounding vegetation turns suddenly from mesquite brush to prickly pear cactus. Further observation shows that this area of prickly pears is actually a swath about a mile wide running from west-southwest to east-northeast. Where did these prickly pears come from? Some area residents believe that they grew from seeds falling from the coats of countless horses, mules, and cattle driven by the Comanches from northern Mexico to their home territory along this route—the **Western Comanche Trace.** Johnson Draw, lying about three miles northeast of the intersection, links Castle Gap (the marker for the Trans-Pecos and Mexico) to Mustang Draw and Big Spring farther east.

To reach **Monahans Sandhills State Park (location of Willow Springs),** take FM 1787 west about 14 miles, to the intersection with SH 385; take SH 385 north about 10 miles to the intersection with IH 20; take IH 20 west about 30 miles to Monahans Sandhills State Park on the north (right) side of IH 20, clearly visible from the highway; take the park road into the dunes area.

Although **Willow Springs** is hidden deep within Monahans Sandhills State Park, the sight of the towering barren sand dunes from the park roads gives the traveler a sense of how special it must have been for anyone—Indian or white—to know of a reliable water source in this desolate area. The sand formations lay over dependable pools of water that break the surface here and there. Wrote one early traveler in the region: "...nothing but sand is to be seen, until...you can see the tops of the Lonely Willow: there is that pure beverage God gave to man."

In 1901, the burnt remains of forty wagons were found near Willow Springs. Local historians believe that the remains were from a wagon train that left Phoenix in 1876 but never reached its destination of St. Louis.

To reach the vicinity of **Ojo de San Martin** from **Monahans Sandhills State Park**, return to IH 20 and proceed west about 43 miles, through the town of Monahans to the U.S. 285 intersection at the town of Pecos; take U.S. 285 north about 40 miles to the FM 652 intersection at the community of Orla; take FM 652 west about 27 miles through the desolate Screw Bean Hills to a highway bridge with a sign that reads, "Delaware River."

Ojo de San Martin lies somewhere at the headwaters of the tiny, improbable Delaware River at an off-road site ten miles or more to the west-southwest of this bridge. The *ojo*, or "eye" (spring), of water was a key stopping place for Indians traveling this harsh country, though it is not known today exactly which of several springs was used; perhaps it was modern Delaware Spring or Independence Spring. Captain Marcy was taken here by his Comanche guide Manuel in 1849 and was so impressed with the waters that he imagined the establishment of a spa like that at Saratoga, New York. The deep, narrow, brush-lined riverbank again gives the viewer a heightened sense of the preciousness of water in such a barren landscape.

Equally improbable as the presence of the river is its direction: Like the Black River in extreme southern New Mexico, twenty-five miles to the north, the Delaware flows east-northeast to join the Pecos. Almost all other significant streams in Texas flow from northwest to southeast. The name *Delaware* is an Indian name, and members of the Delaware tribe pushed westward from their homelands in New Jersey, Pennsylvania, and Delaware after the mid-1700s. In the mid-1800s, they came to Texas and served as expert guides and trackers in the service of the U.S. Army.

Big sky over Guadalupe Peak and Capitan Bluff, the Comanche "gray mountains." Photo by Wayne J. Pate

To reach **Guadalupe Peak** and **Capitan Bluff** from the **Delaware River Bridge** on FM 652, continue west on FM 652 about 14.5 miles to the U.S. 62/180 intersection at the state line of Texas and New Mexico; take U.S. 62/180 west about 18.5 miles to the community of Pine Springs.

Guadalupe Peak was one of the main navigation markers on Indian trips across the region. The peak will come in sight well before reaching the Delaware River Bridge on FM 652. The enormous prehistoric reef known as the Guadalupe Mountains can be seen from as far away as seventy-five miles when the weather is clear. The eastern face of the range rises three thousand feet above the desert floor; it stretches for more than thirty-five miles west of U.S. 62/180, from northeast of Carlsbad Caverns National Park; and it extends almost to the intersection of U.S. 62/180 and Texas SH 54, just below Guadalupe Pass.

Be careful not to mistake the spectacular cliff called **Capitan Bluff** at the southwest end of the range for Guadalupe Peak—the Peak is the rounded, prominent point just north (right) of Capitan Bluff and is actually a few feet higher than the bluff. Even so, Capitan will dominate your attention more and more as you approach Guadalupe Pass, about twelve miles beyond Pine Springs.

Rocks along the cliff face have assumed a gray cast because of weathering, which may be enhanced by the sun's angle and morning mists, leading to the Comanche name for Capitan and the mountains in general, *Esi Toya,* or "Gray Mountain." At 8,749 feet above sea level, Guadalupe Peak is the highest point in Texas, and Pine Springs is the headquarters of Guadalupe Mountains National Park, a complete and memorable vacation in its own right.

To reach a view of the **Salt Basin** from **Guadalupe Peak** and **Capitan Bluff,** continue west on U.S. 62/180 beyond Pine Springs 27 miles, to the community of Salt Flats. The roadway enters Guadalupe Pass and will drop more than 3,000 feet over the course of just a few miles. Excellent vistas are available along this part of the highway; however, extra caution is advised when driving and sightseeing along this section because high winds are prevalent here, and any help for stranded or injured motorists is extremely remote.

The passage through Guadalupe Canyon opens to the immense **Salt Basin.** Lesser mountain ranges unfold to the south, southeast, and west. Huge shining salt beds spread to the south, west, and northwest.

The **Salt Basin** was the bone of contention in one of the most curious feuds in West Texas history. After the Civil War, citizens of the

Capitan Bluff and panorama to the south. Photo by Wayne J. Pate

Hispanic towns along the Rio Grande, principally San Elizario, built a road to the flats and began hauling the salt, which at that time was a valuable commodity not easily obtained. Around the same time, Anglo speculators began laying claim to portions of the salt basin with the intent of closing access to local citizens and developing their own industry.

The issues of ownership and access to the salt became entwined with a number of other volatile matters in regional politics, such as the succession of Mexican law with American law, a competition between the Republican and Democratic parties, and rivalries among individual politicians. The climax was a series of murders and general rioting in the border towns in late 1877, a period aptly called the Salt War. U.S. troops were called in to stop the unrest, and they effectively closed the free salt trade.

These events are significant to Indian history because Tiguas and the descendants of other Pueblo Indians who lived in the river towns were involved in the salt trade and no doubt saw it as a continuation of their traditional, communal rights to resources in the area landscape. For these participants, the end of the Salt War marked another step in the restriction of Indian land use.

To reach a view of **Las Cornudas Mountains** from the **Salt Basin** at Salt Flat, continue west on U.S. 62/180 about 7 miles to the FM 1437 intersection on the north (right) side of the road; take FM 1437 north 13 miles to Dell City; **Las Cornudas Mountains** can be seen from the northern edge of Dell City. They are the prominent hills that are just north of due west of town.

Las Cornudas Mountains, a series of desert peaks (some called by other names), straddle the Texas–New Mexico border. In spite of the fact that they appear almost close enough to touch from the north edge of Dell City, they are more than fifteen miles away—an example of how deceiving distances can be in this region. These hills were a watering place for Randolph Marcy in his Comanche-guided party in 1849 and presumably well known to the Indians. In 1858, the Butterfield stagecoach route followed Marcy's path to the Cornudas watering holes.

The old stage road still exists, running up to the Cornudas across Crow Flats, eight miles east-northeast of Dell City. Somewhere on Crow Flats was the water hole Marcy knew as **Ojo de Cuervo (Crow Springs).** This spring was probably on the west edge of the flats, spilling water into the extensive salt lakes in presettlement times, when the water table was much higher than it is today.

Hueco Tanks. Photo by Daniel J. Gelo

For another view of **Las Cornudas Mountains** en route to **Hueco Tanks,** return south on FM 1437 to the U.S. 62/180 intersection; take U.S. 62/180 west about 16.5 miles, just past the community of Cornudas to the intersection of U.S. 62/180 with FM 2317 on the south (left) side of the road; at this intersection, look just slightly west of due north into the distance; disregard the hills in the foreground, which are part of the Sierra Tinaja Pinta. The most prominent mountain in the distance is San Antonio Peak in the **Cornudas,** the northern slope of which lies across the state line in New Mexico.

To reach **Hueco Tanks State Historical Park** from the community of Cornudas, continue west on U.S. 62/180 about 36 miles to the FM 2775 intersection on the north (right) side of the road; take FM 2775 north about 7 miles to **Hueco Tanks State Historical Park.**

One of the most arresting landscapes in all of Texas, **Hueco Tanks** was a haven for human populations throughout history and prehistory. Hueco Tanks is composed of cliffs and boulders of granitelike rock called *syenite,* and it forms three distinct "mountains." **Hueco Tanks** takes its redundant name from the numerous crevices and hollows (Spanish *huecos*) that store rainwater. The Tanks is an igneous formation begun as magma that pushed toward the surface through limestone sediments thirty-four million years ago. The syenite remained while the softer limestone eroded and the surrounding huge basin formed, and the feature now rises over three hundred feet above the desert floor. Like many of the best Indian campsites, it is a true oasis, harboring plants and animals sustained by the predictable supply of cool water.

Paleo-Indian big-game hunters knew the area about ten thousand years ago, leaving evidence in the form of an occasional Folsom point. The Desert Archaic culture of small-game hunters and plant gatherers followed. After A.D. 600, Hueco Tanks and the surrounding basin were home to Jornado Mogollon villagers. The Mogollon left the majority of pictographs at the Tanks, including over two hundred mask images and plumed serpents, which seem to reflect influences from Aztec Mexico while also anticipating the *kachinas* (masked spirit impersonators) of the historic Pueblo Indians.

A different set of artistic motifs—dancers, warriors with shields, white men, and handprints—were painted by historic period Mescalero Apaches, Comanches, Kiowas, and Tiguas. In all, Hueco Tanks is home to one of the densest collections of Indian pictography on the continent. Experimental photography has recently revealed additional fantastic images done in pigments that are no longer visible to the naked eye.

One can see also see the later graffiti of non-Indian visitors. The Tanks became known to the 49ers crossing Texas, and later (1858–1859) the Butterfield Overland Mail set up a stagecoach stop here—you can still see the trace of the coach road where it crosses the park entrance road right before the main gate. While some of the historic dates and names left on the rocks are interesting, many mar the earlier Indian pictographs.

Picnickers from El Paso frequented the site for most of the twentieth century, often mindless about the damage they were causing to the environment and thus the prehistoric record. In the early 1990s, the Tanks gained fame as a world-class rock climbing site. With climbers arriving from all over the planet in the cool months, degradation increased to the point that access had to be controlled. Self-guided hiking and climbing is now restricted to the North Mountain and is allowed only after a brief orientation at the visitor's center. Camping and guided tours to other areas can be arranged by calling the park headquarters at (915) 849-6684.

Fortunately, some fine rock art remains viewable even in the self-guided areas. From the parking lot on the right of the park road (beyond the visitor's center), take the main trail; bear east, then south, through the gap between North and East Mountains about a quarter-mile to see a long rock shelter containing numerous images, including a snake, a set of dancing figures, and a white man in hat and frock coat. At this shelter and elsewhere, one can also see small hollows in the rock floor that Indians used as mortars for grinding seeds and medicinal plants.

Just beyond this shelter, a small box canyon opens into the northwest face of the East Mountain. Now accessible only by guided tour, this canyon contains Comanche Cave on its southwest wall, the site of a notorious Indian fight. In 1839, about twenty Kiowas, intent on raiding around El Paso, were trapped here by a large Mexican force. For ten days, the Kiowas faced withering fire whenever they attempted to escape or get a drink of water. Some finally got away by climbing a tree through a crevice and running off at night. The story of the siege lives on to this day both in El Paso folklore and Kiowa tribal tradition.

A good view of the little canyon can be gained by climbing the rocks that form the northeast corner of North Mountain and oversee the gap. Start this hike by leaving the parking lot along the pathway marked by log borders; it heads directly toward the nearest rocks. You'll see stanchions and a chain, which aid the climbers that are going high. For the best view of the canyon, however, climb several yards to the west of the stanchions. As you leave the desert floor for the boulders, you will come upon a large shelter; look carefully under the graffiti names for a large white serpent and a mounted warrior with shield and warbonnet, obvious historic Indian pictographs.

Among the boulders ahead and above are more paintings to be discovered, including some wonderful Mogollon masks rendered in red basket-weave geometric patterns on the underside of the huge rocks, which you must view by lying on your back. In viewing the box canyon from the heights of North Mountain, you will notice that a peak looms nine-tenths of a mile beyond in the Hueco Mountains range southeast of the Tanks, precisely marking the otherwise obscure cleft.

Scanning northeast from the same parking lot one views the northeast corner of traditional Tigua deer-hunting territory, marked by the Hueco Mountains across the basin. In particular, Cerro Alto, sixty-nine degrees east of north and 4.4 miles away, was a kind of boundary marker. An imaginary line drawn southeast from Cerro Alto to Small Station (see p. 192) would run through the heart of the hunting grounds, past a number of Tigua rock-shelter camps not accessible by car.

Tigua elders today also remember shooting deer around Los Castillos, the castlelike igneous formation that rises along the foot of the mountains across from the parking lot. From here, the Indians dragged the deer through the low, clear arroyos to be butchered at their Hueco Tanks camps. Also along the southwest face of the Huecos, the Tiguas collected red and yellow pigments for face painting and the decoration of pottery. Perhaps these same sources provided paint for the more ancient artists who adorned the rock wall of Hueco Tanks.

To reach the **Tigua hunting grounds** near **El Paso** from **Hueco Tanks,** return to U.S. 62/180; take U.S. 62/180 west about 9 miles to the Zaragosa Road intersection.

The **sand hills** south of Montana Avenue (U.S. 62) are still apparent in places approaching the Zaragosa Road intersection, despite encroaching subdivisions. They were, until recently, **Tigua hunting territory**. The sand hills were a good place for hunting because every animal's trail is clearly visible in the dunes. Here communal rabbit drives were held. Sometimes the men would put up a strip of wire fencing (an update on the woven netting used in aboriginal times), into which they would drive the rabbits, then club them with wooden clubs called *koas*. Other times, groups of men would pursue rabbits to their holes, dig them out, quickly club them with a koa or shovel, and then toss them over their shoulders into a bag.

A clubbed rabbit would occasionally revive and jump off, startling everyone; other times, a rattlesnake would turn up during the digging instead of a rabbit—again, startling everyone, but perhaps a little more so than the occasional revived rabbit. The women would follow, collecting the rabbits and giving the men a sopapilla or tortilla for each one in ceremonial exchange. The sand hills were also a good location for gathering mesquite firewood, and even today, Tigua people get wood in these areas to burn in their traditional *hornos* (bread ovens).

To reach **La Loma de Barro** from the **sand hills,** take Zaragosa Road south from the U.S. 62 intersection for about 7 miles. View the breaks lying a quarter-mile to the east of the road (now the site of extensive housing development).

The breaks where the desert plateau gives way to the river valley were called **La Loma de Barro** (Clay Hill) by the Tiguas. Here they collected gummy red clay for their pottery from a bed lying below the plateau surface in the arroyos. The original Tigua pottery tradition has faded except for a few revivalists, but through the early years of the twentieth century, the Tiguas' sturdy, undecorated Puebloan ollas were favored by local consumers.

In the 1970s, a tribal factory was established to produce souvenir pottery, made in molds with commercial clay. A variety of shapes and sizes were made, which were then hand-painted using designs and techniques learned from the New Mexico Pueblos, although with some bolder coloration. Samples of the older and newer forms of pottery are on display in various reservation buildings.

To reach **Ysleta del Sur Pueblo (Tigua Indian Reservation)** from **La Loma de Barro,** continue south on Zaragosa Road about 6 miles, past the IH 10 intersection, to the intersection of Zaragosa Road and Socorro Road. The Tigua community consists of several blocks that are east of this intersection. The mission church and casino are in the block adjacent to this intersection to the northeast, and the visitor's center is less than a mile east on Socorro Road, on the right-hand side.

To better appreciate Tigua culture, explore the tribal reservation at Ysleta. An entire community—including the mission church, government buildings, housing, a casino, tribally owned convenience stores, and a visitor's center—portrays the past, present, and future of Indian life in Trans-Pecos Texas.

To reach **Sierra Blanca** from **Ysleta del Sur Pueblo/El Paso,** return north on Zaragosa Road 3 miles to the IH 10 intersection; take IH 10 east toward the town of Sierra Blanca about 75 miles distant. About 26 miles east of the IH 10/Spur 148 intersection exit to Fort Hancock, IH 10 ascends a long mountain pass. Toward the east end of the pass, approaching the large bend where the highway veers southeast, you will note a roadside park on the eastbound lanes. By viewing 36 degrees west of true north from the park, the place 4.9 miles distant and 500 feet below is **Small Station.** The peak of **Sierra Blanca** is visible 3.5 miles north of the highway from just beyond the large bend, and the town of **Sierra Blanca** lies 8.5 miles east of the roadside park on IH 10.

Small Station was essentially the southeast corner of the vast hunting territory roamed by the Tigua Indians out of El Paso from the late 1600s until perhaps the 1960s. The Indians used Small Station as a campsite as well as a landmark. The well-named **Sierra Blanca** (White Mountain) is conspicuous just west of the town with the same name, and it marks the pass between the mountains— the Quitman Mountains on the south and the Finlay Mountains running north.

Note: A major detour is available from this point to **Big Bend.** It departs from **Sierra Blanca** and concludes by returning to IH 10 west of **Gomez Peak.** For this route, proceed now to the section "**Big Bend Detour**" at the end of the chapter (p. 198). Otherwise, continue on the main **Mountains and Basins** route from **Sierra Blanca** to **Gomez Peak.**

> To reach **Gomez Peak** from **Sierra Blanca,** continue on IH 10 from the town of Sierra Blanca about 47 miles to the community of Kent. In this vicinity, Gomez Peak will loom ahead on the south side of the highway. It will stay in view over the next 12 miles as the highway rounds this northern tip of the Davis Mountains, passing to the north and continuing east.

Though appearing barren from this distance, **Gomez Peak** is home to an astounding concentration of active springs, evident from topographic maps. The amount of fresh water here is unlike anything for miles. This abundance of water, plus the position of the peak at the north end of the Davis Range, made it an important landmark for east-west travel. Historical references note that Indians referred to these mountains as Pah-cut, which was probably Comanche *paakatu̲*, "water possessing."

> To reach **Toyah Creek** from **Gomez Peak,** continue east on IH 10 about 30 miles beyond Kent toward the town of Balmorhea; watch for the crossing over **Toyah Creek** 1.7 miles east of the IH 10/FM 2903 intersection.

Toyah Creek was an important location for Indian travelers in the region. Stop at the highway overpass for a brief view of the live, verdant creek. A better sense of this oasis can be had by detouring southwest from IH 10 on SH 17 through the town of Balmorhea and beyond to Balmorhea State Park at Toyahvale.

Several springs feed the system west of the roadway, including Saragosa and Giffin Springs. Just east of the road, the park contains **San Solomon Springs,** which supply the park's spring-fed swimming pool, one of the world's largest. San Solomon Springs has also been called Mescalero Springs, attesting to the presence of Mescalero Apaches, who along with Jumanos drew off springwater for their corn gardens. The headwater reaches of **Toyah Creek** extend south into the Davis Mountains. Toyah *(toya)* means "mountain" in Comanche, and this is one of the very few Comanche placenames that survive in modern Texas geography.

To reach a view of **Lake Leon** from **Toyah Creek,** continue east toward Fort Stockton on IH 10 for about 45 miles; look for the U.S. 67 intersection with IH 10; **Lake Leon** will be just east of this intersection and 0.5 miles south of the IH 10 roadbed (there is a roadside park on the westbound side of the highway opposite the lake).

Lake Leon (Leon Springs Reservoir) was a well-known watering place in Indian days, the site of two enormous natural wells. It later became one of the major stopovers between San Antonio and El Paso for Spanish and Anglo travelers. The present irrigation lake was formed when white settlers dammed the spring outflow, but the springs ceased to flow in the late 1950s and the lake now depends on rain runoff.

To reach **Comanche Springs** from **Lake Leon,** continue east on IH 10 for 8 miles, past Fort Stockton to the U.S. 285 intersection; take U.S. 285 south 0.6 miles to the James Rooney Memorial Park entrance.

On the southeast corner of present Fort Stockton lies the former site of **Comanche Springs.** Six springs here once provided ample water (1,900 liters per second in 1899) and brush for fuel, but the springs went dry in 1961. The underground source of this water was beneath the Glass Mountains some forty miles south of Fort Stockton. The location was also known as Agua Ancha (Broad Water), which was likely a translation of a Comanche name meaning "wide."

The present name was reported to have originated when a party of non-Indian travelers killed a Comanche disguised in a wolf skin as he approached to attack them, but this story may have been a later invention, with the springs simply named for a tribe that frequented the site. The Comanche Trail that led from Horsehead Crossing and into Mexico ran here, and so much Indian livestock was driven past the springs that, according to one early observer, ruts were worn in the solid limestone. Look on the northwest side of Rooney Park where the spring creek runs below a twenty-foot scarp for the place where Indians would have camped.

To reach **Tunas Springs** from **Comanche Springs,** return to IH 10 and continue east for about 20 miles to the roadside park on the eastbound side of the highway.

Tunas (Tunis) Springs, also once called Escondido (Hidden) Springs, lies a quarter-mile south of the roadside park. As the historical marker here notes, traces of a Comanche camp were visible at the springs well into the twentieth century. The spot would not have been obvious to early travelers, but it is locatable with reference to the narrow spur of the enormous Big Mesa, which projects toward the highway from the north and which can be seen across the road from the park. Like many Indian camping places along the San Antonio–El Paso route, Tunas Springs became a stagecoach stop; the station on display here was originally located to the south, closer to the springs.

To reach views of **Darrel's Peak** and **Squawteat Peak** from **Tunas Springs,** continue on IH 10 east. Note **Darrel's Peak** about 3.5 miles east on the south side of the highway. Note **Squawteat Peak** about 10.5 miles east of **Darrel's Peak** on the north side of the highway.

Darrel's Peak aligns with Tunas Springs to the west and Squawteat Peak to the east. Though Indian use of Darrel's Peak is not established, it was probably a native landmark showing the trail past the "hidden" springs for westward travelers. **Squawteat Peak** rises 280 feet above the roadbed just west of Bakersfield. Its unfortunate name only suggests, and does not verify, its role as an Indian landmark during the historic period; however, it, too, likely marked the path along Tunas Creek past Tunas Springs. It can be seen for many miles from the east, aligning with Darrel's Peak to the west, just east of the springs.

The name *squawteat* may have originated from an Indian word, since the Indian practice of referring to certain mountains as "breast mountain" and the like was widespread, perhaps originally an allusion to Mother Earth. There is a "breast mountain" in southwest Oklahoma where the Comanches live today, and similar place-names are found in the Rocky Mountains and the Great Basin, homelands of the Comanches' ancestors.

Extensive archaeological work around the base of the Texas peak, begun when IH 10 was extended in 1974, definitely confirms more ancient Indian activity here. A large midden (stone mound for

Squawteat Peak. Photo by Daniel J. Gelo

processing vegetable foods) was discovered and carbon-dated to about 1300, part of a huge campsite with many distinct subareas and abundant artifacts, including tools and the rings left by *wickiups* (brush dwellings).

To reach **Horsehead Crossing** from **Squawteat Peak,** return west on IH 10 past the Tunas Springs roadside park about 6.5 miles to the SH 67 intersection; take SH 67 north 32 miles to the SH 11 intersection at Girvin; take SH 11 north about 12 miles; look for a caliche road that veers off the pavement to the right at a 60-degree angle (10 degrees east of north), and look for a sign that reads simply, "Historical Marker, 4 Miles"; follow the caliche road approximately 4 miles to reach **Horsehead Crossing.**

Before West Texas was heavily settled, the Pecos River was so deep and powerful that it could be crossed with relative safety at only a few places. Such a place was **Horsehead Crossing.** The **Western Comanche Trace** crossed here. On their return from northern

Horsehead Crossing with Castle Gap on the horizon. Photo by Wayne J. Pate

Mexico, Comanches drove back thousands of horses, mules, and cattle that they had captured on their raids. Though they were weak from having been driven long ways with little water, the animals ran headlong as they smelled the river. Those that arrived at the banks out of control sated themselves but then frequently died from drinking too much too fast. Scores of horse skeletons marked the spot, and their skulls were the most memorable part of the grim scene, resulting in the place-name. Other tribes and non-Indian settlers were also familiar with the site, and it became the location of ambushes and gunfights.

The **Mountains and Basins** route has now come full circle: looking east-northeast from **Horsehead Crossing,** see **Castle Mountain** and **Castle Gap** about 12 miles away.

BIG BEND DETOUR

The Big Bend area is treated as a detour for a couple of reasons. First, while it is undoubtedly an area that saw significant Indian use, Big Bend lay south of the generally east-west path of non-Indian travel; and so, less detailed information about Indian activity here has passed into the historical record than in other areas of the state. Second, because this vast area includes a national park but otherwise few public accommodations, it deserves separate travel planning.

The following is a long and richly scenic ride through the Big Bend country off of the main Mountains and Basins route. This tour can be divided into any number of shorter alternate routes by consulting a standard road map. Several confirmed Indian landmarks can also be included in a visit to the area.

To reach **Big Bend** from **Sierra Blanca** (leaving the main Mountains and Basins route), continue east on IH 10 about 33 miles to the U.S. 90 intersection at Van Horn; take U.S. 90 east (south) about 74 miles through Valentine and on to the U.S. 67 intersection at Marfa; take U.S. 67 south about 59 miles through Shafter to the SH 170 intersection at Presidio (on the U.S.–Mexico border); take SH 170 about 67.5 miles through Terlingua to the SH 118 intersection; continue east/south on SH 118 into **Big Bend National Park.**

To reach **Gomez Peak** from **Big Bend** (returning to the main Mountains and Basins route) take U.S. 385 north from the SH 118 intersection at Panther Junction about 69 miles to the U.S. 67/90

Rio Grande along River Road. Photo by Wayne J. Pate

intersection at Marathon; take U.S. 67/90 west about 30 miles to the SH 118 intersection at Alpine; take SH 118 north about 77 miles through Fort Davis to the IH 10 intersection at Kent.

Nearly opposite Presidio, the Rio Conchos flows out of Chihuahua to join the Rio Grande. This river junction is called **La Junta de los Rios,** and it was the fertile center of village life for the Jumanos and associated peoples during the 1600s and earlier. Much of the two-lane highway SH 170, or "River Road," runs within sight of the Rio Grande, showing the contrast of a band of green riparian land cutting through desolate mountains that would have been appealing to native travelers and gardeners.

For most of this stretch, River Road passes through the southern edge of **Big Bend Ranch State Park,** a preserve nearly as large as **Big Bend National Park** directly east. A number of Western movies have been filmed in this vicinity, and it is easy to imagine the sound of hoof beats echoing in the canyons. This area is also a geological wonderland, the destination of student bus trips from all the major Texas universities.

Lajitas on SH 170 is the likely site of the **Comanche Pass** or San Carlos Crossing, a major Indian ford. From the ford, Indians went to San Carlos, Coahuila, ten miles south to secure guns and ammunition for their southerly raids. Southeast of Lajitas, the Rio Grande passes through **Santa Elena Canyon** and then **Mariscal Canyon** and **Boquillas Canyon,** which were other gathering places for Apache, Comanche, and Kiowa raiders heading into Mexico on the **Western Comanche Trace** during the 1800s.

Another key Indian ford—called El Vado de Chisos, or Gran Pasos de los Indios (Grand Indian Crossing)—was at the head or tail of one of these canyons, but its exact location is now uncertain. The Indians would arrive in the area from Horsehead Crossing and Comanche Springs along the section of trace known as the **Chisos Trail,** and from this point, they moved to campsites deep in Coahuila and Chihuahua. Among the historic tribes named, only some bands of the Apaches stayed in the area mountains regularly. The Apache leader Victorio may have hidden here in his desperate attempts to evade capture by the U.S. Army during the 1880s.

Within the National Park are some definite Indian camping places. One Comanche Trail campsite was **Neville Springs,** in a deep ravine 3.6 miles directly north of Panther Junction, approachable 1.2 miles east of Government Spring Road, 4.5 miles north of Basin Junction. U.S. Army Black Seminole scouts were stationed at a camp here in the 1880s to control Apache and Mexican bandit traffic.

At **Boquillas Hot Springs,** two miles directly west of Rio Grande Village, prehistoric Indians dug a bathing pit to take advantage of the steaming flow. In 1747, the Spanish observed Apaches gardening at this location, and Comanches later used the place as a trail stop. Another water source on the Comanche Trail was **Glenn Spring** (also called Jordan Spring) about eleven miles southsoutheast of Panther Junction or about ten miles almost due west of Boquillas Hot Springs, at the southern foot of Chilicotal Mountain.

Guidebooks for other specific points of interest in the park are readily available in most major bookstores in Texas, as well as at the park headquarters and at Chisos Basin Lodge.

When heading north from the National Park, another Comanche Trail water hole is found at **Peña Colorado Springs,** which lie in a park at the end of Post Road running about five miles south from Marathon. These springs were also the site of prehistoric Indian occupations, many of which are now underwater in the park lake. From Marathon, the detour runs to Alpine (visit **Kokernot Spring,** an Apache water hole, in the park on the northeast side of town) and then north through the beautiful Davis Mountains, rugged country that Native travelers knew for its abundance of water.

BIBLIOGRAPHY

Armbruster, Henry C. *The Torreys of Texas.* Buda, Tex.: Citizen Press, 1968.

Aston, B. W., and Donathan Taylor. *Along the Texas Forts Trail.* Denton, Tex.: University of North Texas Press, 1997.

Aten, Lawrence E. *Indians of the Upper Texas Coast.* New York: Academic Press, 1983.

Awbrey, Betty Dooley, Clause Dooley, and the Texas Historical Commission. *Why Stop? A Guide to Texas Historical Roadside Markers.* Houston: Gulf Publishing, 1978.

Baker, James H., and Raymond E. Cage II. *The Indians in the History of Tarrant County, Texas.* Fort Worth: Tarrant County Archaeological Society, 1962.

Baker, T. Lindsay. *Ghost Towns of Texas.* Norman: University of Oklahoma Press, 1986.

Bedichek, Roy. *Karánkaway Country.* Austin: University of Texas Press, 1974.

Berlandier, Jean Louis. *The Indians of Texas in 1830.* Ed. John C. Ewers. Washington, D.C.: Smithsonian Institution Press, 1969.

Bieber, Ralph P., and Averam B. Bender, eds. *Exploring Southwestern Trails, 1846–1854.* Glendale, Calif.: The Arthur H. Clark Company, 1938.

Bomar, George W. *Texas Weather.* Austin: University of Texas Press, 1983.

Brice, Donaly E. *The Great Comanche Raid.* Austin: Eakin Press, 1987.

Brown, John Henry. *Indian Wars and Pioneers of Texas.* Austin: L. E. Daniell, n.d.

Brune, Gunnar. *Springs of Texas.* Fort Worth: Branch-Smith, 1982.

Campbell, T. N. "The Payaya Indians of Southern Texas." Southern Texas Archaeological Association, Special Publication No. 1, 1975.

Campbell, T. N., and T. J. Campbell. "Historic Indian Groups of the Choke Canyon Reservoir and Surrounding Area, Southern Texas." University of Texas at San Antonio Center for Archaeological Research, Choke Canyon Series, vol. 1, 1981.

Campbell, T. N., and William T. Field. "Identification of Comanche Raiding Trails in Trans-Pecos Texas." *West Texas Historical Association Year Book* 44 (October 1968), pp. 128–144.

Carroll, H. Bailey. "Nolan's 'Lost Nigger' Expedition of 1877." *Southwestern Historical Quarterly* 44:1 (July 1940), pp. 55–75.

Cherokee County History. Jacksonville, Tex.: Cherokee County Historical Commission, 1986.

Clarke, May Whatley. *Chief Bowles and the Texas Cherokees.* Norman: University of Oklahoma Press, 1971.

Cook, John R. *The Border and the Buffalo.* Austin: State House Press, 1989.

Costello, David F. *The Prairie World.* New York: Thomas Y. Crowell, 1969.

Dearen, Patrick. *Castle Gap and the Pecos Frontier.* Fort Worth: Texas Christian University Press, 1988.

Doughty, Robin W. *Wildlife and Man in Texas.* College Station: Texas A&M University Press, 1983.

Everett, Dianna. *The Texas Cherokees: A People between Two Fires, 1819–1840.* Norman: University of Oklahoma Press, 1990.

Flores, Dan L. *Journal of an Indian Trader: Anthony Glass and the Texas Trading Frontier, 1790–1810.* College Station: Texas A&M University Press, 1985.

———. *Caprock Canyonlands.* Austin: University of Texas Press, 1990.

———. *Horizontal Yellow: Nature and History in the Near Southwest.* Albuquerque: University of New Mexico Press, 1999.

Foreman, Grant. *Marcy and the Gold Seekers.* Norman: University of Oklahoma Press, 1939.

———, ed. *Adventure on Red River.* Norman: University of Oklahoma Press, 1937.

Foster, William C., and Jack Jackson. "The 1693 Expedition of Gregorio de Salinas Varona to Sustain the Missionaries among the Tejas Indians." *Southwestern Historical Quarterly* 97:3 (January 1993), pp. 264–311.

Francaviglia, Richard V. *The Cast Iron Forest: A Natural and Cultural History of the North American Cross Timbers.* Austin: University of Texas Press, 2000.

Gadus, Eloise F., and Margaret Ann Howard. *Hunter-Fisher-Gatherers on the Upper Texas Coast: Archaeological Investigations at the Peggy Lake Disposal Area, Harris County, Texas.* Reports of Investigations No. 74. Austin, Tex.: Prewitt and Associates, 1990.

Gelo, Daniel J. "Recalling the Past in Creating the Present: Topographic References in Comanche Narrative." *Western Folklore* 53:4 (October 1994), pp. 295–312.

———. "'Comanche Land and Ever Has Been': A Native Geography of the Nineteenth Century Comanchería." *Southwestern Historical Quarterly* 103:3 (January 2000), pp. 273–308.

Guthrie, Keith. *History of San Patricio County.* Austin: Nortex, 1986.

Hacker, Margaret S. *Cynthia Ann Parker: The Life and the Legend.* El Paso: Texas Western Press, 1990.

Haley, J. Evetts. *Fort Concho and the Texas Frontier.* San Angelo, Tex.: San Angelo Standard-Times, 1952.

———. *The XIT Ranch and the Early Days of the Llano Estacado.* Norman: University of Oklahoma Press, 1967.

Hedrick, John A. "Investigations of Tigua Potters and Pottery at Ysleta del Sur, Texas." *The Artifact* 9:2 (1971), pp. 1–17.

Hickerson, Nancy Parrott. *The Jumanos: Hunters and Traders of the South Plains.* Austin: University of Texas Press, 1994.

Himmel, Kelly F. *The Conquest of the Karankawas and the Tonkawas, 1821–1859.* College Station: Texas A&M University Press, 1999.

Howard, James H. *Shawnee! The Ceremonialism of a Native Indian Tribe and Its Cultural Background.* Athens, Ohio: Ohio University Press, 1981.

Howard, Margaret Ann, and Martha Doty Freeman. *Inventory and Assessment of Cultural Resources at Bear Creek Park, Addicks Reservoir, Harris County, Texas.* Reports of Investigations No. 24. Austin, Tex.: Prewitt and Associates, 1983.

Hunt, Steven M. *Cultural Resources Survey of the Proposed California Lane Neighborhood Park, City of Arlington, Tarrant County, Texas.* Miscellaneous Reports of Investigations No. 203. Plano, Tex.: Geo-Marine, 2000.

Kenner, Charles L. *A History of New Mexican-Plains Indian Relations.* Norman: University of Oklahoma Press, 1969.

———. *The Comanchero Frontier.* Norman: University of Oklahoma Press, 1994.

Kirkland, Forrest, and W. W. Newcomb Jr. *The Rock Art of Texas Indians.* Austin: University of Texas Press, 1996.

Latorre, Felipe A., and Dolores L. Latorre. *The Mexican Kickapoo Indians.* New York: Dover, 1991.

Lehmann, Herman. *Nine Years among the Indians, 1870–1879.* Albuquerque: University of New Mexico Press, 1993.

Loyd, Doyal T. *A History of Upshur County.* Gilmer, Tex.: Gilmer *Mirror,* 1966.

Martin, Howard. "Texas Redskins in Confederate Gray." *Southwestern Historical Quarterly* 70:4 (April 1967), pp. 586–592.

————. "Polk County Indians: Alabamas, Coushattas, Pakana Muskogees." *East Texas Historical Journal* 17:1 (Spring 1979), pp. 3–23.

McWhorter, Eugene W. *Traditions of the Land: The History of Gregg County.* Longview, Tex.: Gregg County Historical Foundation, 1989.

Morris, John Miller. *El Llano Estacado.* Austin: University of Texas Press, 1997.

Newcomb, W. W., Jr. *The Indians of Texas: From Prehistoric to Modern Times.* Austin: University of Texas Press, 1961.

Nunn, W. Curtis. "Eighty-Six Hours without Water on the Texas Plains." *Southwestern Historical Quarterly* 43:3 (January 1940), pp. 356–364.

Nye, Wilbur Sturtevant. *Carbine and Lance: The Story of Old Fort Sill.* Norman: University of Oklahoma Press, 1969.

Pecos County Historical Commission. *Pecos County History.* 2 vols. Canyon, Tex.: Staked Plains Press, 1984.

A Pictorial History of Polk County, Texas, 1846–1910. Rev. ed. Livingston, Tex.: Polk County Bicentennial Commission, 1978.

Pittman, Blair, and William A. Owens. *The Natural World of the Texas Big Thicket.* College Station: Texas A&M University Press, 1978.

Pool, William C. *A History of Bosque County.* San Marcos, Tex.: San Marcos Record Press, 1954.

————. *Bosque Territory: A History of an Agrarian Community.* Kyle, Tex.: Chapparal Press, 1964.

Rathjen, Frederick W. *The Texas Panhandle Frontier.* Lubbock: Texas Tech University Press, 1998.

Reitz, Robert, and Gardner Smith. *Medicine Mounds.* Oak Cliff, Tex.: The Sun and Shadow Press, 2000.

Richardson, Rupert. *The Comanche Barrier to South Plains Settlement.* New York: Kraus Reprints, 1973.

Ricklis, Robert A. *The Karankawa Indians of Texas: An Ecological Study of Cultural Tradition and Change.* Austin: University of Texas Press, 1996.

The Roads of Texas. Fredericksburg, Tex.: Shearer Publishing, 1999.

Robertson, Pauline Durrett, and R. L. Robertson. *Tascosa: Historic Site in the Texas Panhandle.* Amarillo: Paramount Publishing Company, 1977.

Roemer, Erwin. *Facts about Artifacts.* Austin: Texas Parks and Wildlife, 1998.

Shafer, Harry J. *Ancient Texans: Rock Art and Lifeways along the Lower Pecos.* Austin: Texas Monthly Press, 1986.

Smith, F. Todd. *The Caddo Indians: Tribes at the Convergence of Empire, 1542–1854*. College Station: Texas A&M University Press, 1995.

————. *The Wichita Indians: Traders of Texas and the Southern Plains, 1540–1845*. College Station: Texas A&M University Press, 2000.

Stephens, A. Ray, and William M. Holmes. *Historical Atlas of Texas*. Norman: University of Oklahoma Press, 1989.

Sutherland, Kay. *Rock Paintings at Hueco Tanks Historical State Park*. Austin: Texas Parks and Wildlife Press, 1995.

Tales and Trails of Bailey County: The First Seventy Years, 1918–1988. Muleshoe, Tex.: Bailey County History Book Committee, 1988.

Taylor, Ira Thomas. *The Cavalcade of Jackson County*. San Antonio: Naylor Company, 1938.

Texas Atlas & Gazetteer. Yarmouth, Maine: DeLorme Publishing, 2000.

Texas Historical Commission. *The New Handbook of Texas*. 6 vols. Austin: Texas State Historical Association, 1996.

Texas State Travel Guide. Austin: Texas Department of Transportation, n.d.

Timanus, Rod. *An Illustrated History of Texas Forts*. Plano, Tex.: Republic of Texas Press, 2001.

Tolbert, Francis X. *The Staked Plain*. Dallas: Southern Methodist University Press, 1987.

Wallace, Ernest. "The Journal of Ranald S. Mackenzie's Messenger to the Kwahadi Comanches." *Red River Valley Historical Review* 3:2 (Spring 1978), pp. 227–246.

Walter, Ray A. *A History of Limestone County*. Austin: Von Boeckmann-Jones, 1959.

Weslager, C. A. *The Delaware Indians: A History*. New Brunswick, N.J.: Rutgers University Press, 1972.

Wheat, Joe Ben. *The Addicks Dam Site: An Archaeological Survey of the Addicks Dam Basin, Southeast Texas*. Bureau of American Ethnology Bulletin 154, pp. 143–152. Washington, D.C.: U.S. Government Printing Office, 1953.

Wilbarger, J. W. *Indian Depredations in Texas*. Austin: Eakin Press, 1985.

Winfrey, Dorman H., and James M. Day. *The Indian Papers of Texas and the Southwest, 1825–1916*. 5 vols. Austin: Texas State Historical Association, 1995.

Wright, Bill. *The Tiguas: Pueblo Indians of Texas*. El Paso: Texas Western Press, 1993.

Wright, Bill, and E. John Gesick Jr. *The Texas Kickapoo: Keepers of Tradition*. El Paso: Texas Western Press, 1996.

Wright, Muriel H. *Guide to the Indian Tribes of Oklahoma*. Norman: University of Oklahoma Press, 1951.

INDEX

Page numbers in italics indicate maps.

OTHER A TO Z GUIDES FROM
THE SCARECROW PRESS, INC.

1. *The A to Z of Buddhism* by Charles S. Prebish, 2001.
2. *The A to Z of Catholicism* by William J. Collinge, 2001.
3. *The A to Z of Hinduism* by Bruce M. Sullivan, 2001.
4. *The A to Z of Islam* by Ludwig W. Adamec, 2002.
5. *The A to Z of Slavery & Abolition* by Martin A. Klein, 2002.
6. *Terrorism: Assassins to Zealots* by Sean Kendall Anderson and Stephen Sloan, 2003.
7. *The A to Z of the Korean War* by Paul M. Edwards, 2005.
8. *The A to Z of the Cold War* by Joseph Smith and Simon Davis, 2005.
9. *The A to Z of the Vietnam War* by Edwin E. Moise, 2005.
10. *The A to Z of Science Fiction Literature* by Brian Stableford, 2005.
11. *The A to Z of the Holocaust* by Jack R. Fischel, 2005.
12. *The A to Z of Washington, D.C.* by Robert Benedetto, Jane Donovan, and Kathleen DuVall, 2005.
13. *The A to Z of Taoism* by Julian F. Pas, 2006.
14. *The A to Z of the Renaissance* by Charles G. Nauert, 2006.
15. *The A to Z of Shinto* by Stuart D. B. Picken, 2006.
16. *The A to Z of Byzantium* by John H. Rosser, 2006.
17. *The A to Z of the Civil War* by Terry L. Jones, 2006.
18. *The A to Z of the Friends (Quakers)* by Margery Post Abbott, Mary Ellen Chijioke, Pink Dandelion, and John William Oliver Jr., 2006
19. *The A to Z of Feminism* by Janet K. Boles and Diane Long Hoeveler, 2006.
20. *The A to Z of New Religious Movements* by George D. Chryssides, 2006.
21. *The A to Z of Multinational Peacekeeping* by Terry M. Mays, 2006.
22. *The A to Z of Lutheranism* by Günther Gassmann with Duane H. Larson and Mark W. Oldenburg, 2007.
23. *The A to Z of the French Revolution* by Paul R. Hanson, 2007.
24. *The A to Z of the Persian Gulf War 1990–1991* by Clayton R. Newell, 2007.
25. *The A to Z of Revolutionary America* by Terry M. Mays, 2007.
26. *The A to Z of the Olympic Movement* by Bill Mallon with Ian Buchanan, 2007.

55. *The A to Z of the War of 1812* by Robert Malcomson, 2009.
56. *The A to Z of Feminist Philosophy* by Catherine Villanueva Gardner, 2009.
57. *The A to Z of the Early American Republic* by Richard Buel Jr., 2009.
58. *The A to Z of the Russo–Japanese War* by Rotem Kowner, 2009.
59. *The A to Z of Anglicanism* by Colin Buchanan, 2009.
60. *The A to Z of Scandinavian Literature and Theater* by Jan Sjåvik, 2009.
61. *The A to Z of the Peoples of the Southeast Asian Massif* by Jean Michaud, 2009.
62. *The A to Z of Judaism* by Norman Solomon, 2009.
63. *The A to Z of the Berbers (Imazighen)* by Hsain Ilahiane, 2009.
64. *The A to Z of British Radio* by Seán Street, 2009.
65. *The A to Z of The Salvation Army* by Major John G. Merritt, 2009.
66. *The A to Z of the Arab–Israeli Conflict* by P R Kumaraswamy, 2009.
67. *The A to Z of the Jacksonian Era and Manifest Destiny* by Terry Corps, 2009.
68. *The A to Z of Socialism* by Peter Lamb and James C. Docherty, 2009.
69. *The A to Z of Marxism* by David Walker and Daniel Gray, 2009.
70. *The A to Z of the Bahá'í Faith* by Hugh C. Adamson, 2009.
71. *The A to Z of Postmodernist Literature and Theater* by Fran Mason, 2009.
72. *The A to Z of Australian Radio and Television* by Albert Moran and Chris Keating, 2009.
73. *The A to Z of the Lesbian Liberation Movement: Still the Rage* by JoAnne Myers, 2009.
74. *The A to Z of the United States–Mexican War* by Edward H. Moseley and Paul C. Clark Jr., 2009.
75. *The A to Z of World War I* by Ian V. Hogg, 2009.
76. *The A to Z of World War II: The War Against Japan* by Anne Sharp Wells, 2009.
77. *The A to Z of Witchcraft* by Michael D. Bailey, 2009.
78. *The A to Z of British Intelligence* by Nigel West, 2009.
79. *The A to Z of United States Intelligence* by Michael A. Turner, 2009.